Skunk

Animal

Series editor: Jonathan Burt

Skunk

Alyce Miller

REAKTION BOOKS

This book is dedicated to my beloved sister Letitia

Published by
REAKTION BOOKS LTD
Unit 32, Waterside
44–48 Wharf Road
London N1 7UX, UK
www.reaktionbooks.co.uk

First published 2015

Printed in India by Replika Press Pvt. Ltd.

A catalogue record for this book is available from the British Library

ISBN 978 1 78023 490 8

Contents

Introduction

What's black and white and stinks all over?

Depending on whom you ask, mention of skunks elicits strong reactions. Symbolic of cuteness or humour in logos and cartoons, skunks are simultaneously loathed in person, fetid figures of the abject. They can be hero, nuisance or farmer's friend. Conflicting adjectives from vicious and dangerous to adorable and affectionate compose a paradoxical picture. Much to the skunk's detriment, negative associations often win out over the facts.

Despite their physical beauty, skunks are not usually depicted in the more serious visual arts. With few exceptions, neither have they served as august symbols in literature. Skunks don't typically star in movies, they aren't raced or fought, and social protocols of elite sports hunting don't include ritualized 'skunk hunts'. Although skunk fur coats have gone through periods of popularity, skunk meat has never been a first-choice entrée on a restaurant menu. Even with an active subculture of skunk pet owners and devotees, skunks still don't top the list of animal companions. Skunks have played a far less glamorous role in human relations and contemplations than have many of their animal peers. Unlike the graceful swan, the skunk is not celebrated in serious music, nor represented in dance. The skunk is no match in cultural and aesthetic cachet for the awe-inspiring power of big cats or the theatricality in fables and fairy tales of wolves and foxes. Though visually dramatic in their rich black-and-white coats, they are

A fearless skunk pauses midway across the road.

7

Skunk family happily browses a backyard for insects.

unsung compared to other black-and-white animals: the zebra with its breathtaking symmetry, or the anthropomorphized tuxedo-wearing penguin.

Unlike dogs, with whom we have co-evolved, skunks share no long history with humans. Nor have they inspired the same amount of evolutionary curiosity as, say, the great apes.

Despite their stinky reputations, skunks are commendable for their individualistic natures and preference for solitude, along with their contentment to hang in the wings, allowing others to take centre stage.

However, it turns out that skunks are amazing animals, and the truths about them explode the myths. Some wildlife researchers have opined that skunks may win the prize for the most misunderstood mammals of North America.[1] Misconceptions have arisen for various reasons, perhaps starting with the interchangeable use of 'polecat' for both the New World skunk and the

European polecat, which resulted in mistakenly attributing to New World skunks the polecat's particular nasty habit of destroying poultry and game.[2]

What follows here is both exploration and celebration of the skunk's understated presence in the New World. Animal species valued by human beings typically are appreciated for anthropomorphic characteristics prized among *Homo sapiens*: good looks, brains, power, sociability, loyalty, companionship. But none of these valued features typically springs to mind when skunks are invoked. In fact, the very mention of skunks is more likely to prompt disgust and reference to an unfortunate encounter. This is because most people experience skunks only from inhaling invisible wafts of their musky odour, and this usually from skunks who have met the same fate as many of their brethren – death by motorized vehicle.

Curious baby deer investigating gentle skunk kits.

Given the abundant misinformation about these intriguing animals, skunks have undeservedly acquired bad reputations. Sometimes perceived as secretive and furtive, and even feared as dangerous both for their spray and as perceived primary vectors of rabies, skunks are often treated as 'nuisance animals'. But humans who take the time to know skunks offer a much more elaborate picture, offsetting the hype of odious peril and rabies-induced hydrophobic danger.

Shortly after I began this book, one of my house cats awoke from napping in his inside window perch to the sight of his nemesis, the fluffy black-and-white neighbour cat, slinking through the yew bushes by the porch. To quell my cat's agitated yowls, I zipped out the door to chase off the trespasser. Bushy tail? Check. White-and-black body? Check. Belly-creeping along the underbrush in pursuit of small prey? Check. But in that split second before I started clapping loudly, the intruder turned his head to look at me. Instead of the round, gold-eyed face of the neighbour's cat, I found myself staring into the small buttony eyes of a large skunk, so breathtakingly beautiful in his feathery black-and-white pelage that I forgot about my distraught cat at the window. Without missing a beat, the undaunted skunk returned to business and continued his leisurely amble through the ivy. Unfazed by my presence, he took his time, eventually disappearing behind a rotting old silver maple stump at the edge of the yard.

Like the amorous cartoon character Pepé Le Pew (who we meet in chapter Seven), who mistakes the cat Penelope for his perfect skunk femme fatale, I believed I had barely escaped my own 'fatal' encounter, but of the reverse kind. Assuming that my mis-recognition was a close call, I reported the anecdote with great zeal over the next few days. But the truth was that, even as close and noisy as I had been, the skunk gave no indication he had done anything but register my presence, before moving on.

Later in the same week, my dog and I set out for our evening walk, when another foraging skunk crossed our path. This time, there was no mistaking the familiar amble and the long plume of tail. This skunk's coat was almost all white, his luxurious fur shimmering like new-fallen snow under the rays of the street lamp. Just beyond, another evening stroller hurried to cross the street, shouting out in warning, 'Skunk! You better watch out! That skunk glared at me!' When I didn't respond, he turned on his heel to hasten off into the darkness.

My dog and I paused for another minute, watching the beautiful – dare I say, regal – white skunk continue across a front lawn, completely undaunted. Then, like a liquid shadow, he vanished magically under a bush and into the night.

Soon after I agreed to write this book, the frequency and intensity of my encounters with skunks began to increase, mostly after dusk, as if word had spread and they were showing up to lobby for a more balanced representation. Friends and neighbours have

Mama skunk carefully escorts her kit across a road to safety. Traffic is the main cause of skunk mortality.

11

been generous with their excited reports of skunk sightings as well, which have often led to questions addressed in this book. Urban sprawl and encroaching human development have meant habitat loss and fragmentation, creating the phenomenon known as 'urban wildlife'. Skunks coexist with animals like white-tailed deer, rabbits, coyotes, foxes, raccoons, possums and bobcats, all of whom are in increasingly closer contact with humans.[3]

What can we learn about the often stigmatized skunk, and what does the skunk have to teach us? The PBS documentary film *Is That Skunk?* opened an important door to the inner life of the skunk, briefly placing a spotlight on a fascinating animal.[4] Viewers have expressed surprise and pleasure at having their misconceptions of skunks challenged.

I, too, experienced surprise and pleasure when one Saturday afternoon six orphaned baby skunk visitors arrived by appointment at my house in Bloomington, Indiana. They were carried in an innocuous plastic travel case held in the grip of a local wildlife rehabilitation specialist. It was hard to believe that six skunks were hiding inside. But as soon as the carrier door was flung open, they all popped out, like the famous clown-car circus trick. Curious and excited, they rippled along, fast as quicksilver, flashing various patterns of black and white. For the next few hours, my two cats and dog observed, transfixed, through the screen door, following the antics of the six kits who roamed the yard with the two humans in hot pursuit, corralling them from trouble. The orphans' mother had been shot by a farmer who discovered her nesting under his house. This is an all-too-familiar story. To the farmer's credit, when he realized he had killed a nursing mother, he contacted the wildlife rehabilitator.

Long after my striped guests had departed, their essence lingered – a rich, earthy scent that brings us closer to the wild. Skunks are actually very clean animals, but the scent of these

A litter of enthusiastic baby skunk visitors, orphaned by a shotgun, exploring the author's home and leaving behind the remarkable gift of scent that keeps on giving.

babies was stronger without a mother attending to their hygiene.

Skunks can help us think about how and why strong human attitudes develop around particular animals – historically, culturally and aesthetically – and what the consequences are for the animals themselves. Animal advocacy is on the rise, bolstering legal protections for animals both domestic and wild. Human understanding of this relatively unheralded animal may contribute to the skunk's well-being, and to our own.

Skunks may be some of the most elusive and misconstrued native animals, but they are also among the most beautiful, intelligent, curious and amiable, with an interesting history. Mostly solitary and peace-loving, skunks readily adapt from forest and meadow to urban and suburban landscapes. Skunks conduct themselves with a certain grace, aplomb and rectitude. Historically misplaced by scientists into the weasel family, mythologized by Native Americans as both villain and saviour, slaughtered for their beautiful fur and the famous scent glands used for perfume musk, considered either exotic or revolting as a food source, notorious for their malodorous defence mechanism, and beloved by many as affectionate and inquisitive pets, skunks offer an opportunity for considering more deeply the complicated relationships between human and non-human animals.

1 Historical Skunk

Alongside magnificent Galápagos tortoises and silky-fleeced alpaca, skunks of the Americas can also lay claim to being bona fide New World animals. American author and wildlife artist Ernest Thompson Seton (a founder of the Boy Scouts of America) dubs the striped skunk 'the proper emblem of America'. The 'profound admiration' he expresses for the skunk incorporates a gently nationalistic sentiment:

> It is, first of all, peculiar to this continent. It has stars on its head and stripes on its body. It is an ideal citizen; minds its own business, harms no one, and is habitually inoffensive, as long as it is left alone; but it will face any one or any number when aroused.[1]

Appreciation for the skunk's confident nature surfaces in this paean by American biologist and conservationist H. E. Anthony (1890–1970):

> It [the skunk] is perfectly fearless of man and other animals, and if allowed to go its way undisturbed, will pass close to you with a genteel and dignified indifference, attending strictly to its own business; but, if interfered with or followed closely or suddenly alarmed, it will

European explorers making first contact in the 'New World' with Native peoples, while bearing flags and religion.

prepare for self protection, and woe to the man or animal insisting on disturbing it too much. Such implicit confidence has the animal in its own ability to defend itself that it wanders about as boldly as though lord of all it surveys.[2]

Skunks were among the first exotic creatures recorded in the annals of early European explorers engaged in Western discovery and conquest. For many, the skunk was another example of the strangeness of this novel land. But skunks were already well known to Native populations of the Americas. Some kept domesticated skunks as animal companions; others valued wild skunks for their skills in agricultural pest control. Many Native Americans found much to honour in the skunk's unique beauty and powerful qualities and, for some tribes, the skunk was even revered as a 'spirit guide' and a clan animal.

Two centuries after Christopher Columbus described scores of New World animals, evidently including skunks, the British explorer and naturalist John Lawson detailed skunks among the strange fauna he observed in his travels, beginning in 1700, in the mid-Atlantic region of 'Carolina'. In addition to his startling claim of having seen a 'tyger' (he most likely meant a jaguar), Lawson offered observations on the skunk that illustrate as much about the cultural and social mindset of the explorer himself as they do about skunks:

Polcats or Skunks in *America,* are different from those in *Europe.* They are thicker, and of a great many Colours; not all alike, but each differing from another in the particular Colour. They smell like a Fox, but ten times stronger. When a Dog encounters them, they piss upon him, and he will

New World iguanas, like many of the animals that explorers have encountered, are reimagined and depicted as monstrous and even mythical.

not be sweet again in a Fortnight or more. The *Indians* love to eat their flesh, which has no manner of ill Smell, when the Bladder is out. I know no use their Furs are put to. They are easily brought up tame.[3]

Lawson wasn't the only one whose well-intentioned reportage about the new land was sometimes skewed or incomplete. Misconceptions sprang up about the people, plants and animals these European arrivals were encountering. Amazing first-hand accounts documented by Spanish explorer Gonzalo Fernández de Oviedo y Valdés (1475–1557) in *Natural and General History of the Indies* (see chapter Three) were no exception. Chronicling sightings of such creatures as mermen and griffins, Oviedo focused briefly on *zorillas* (skunks) and asserted their ability to transmit the terrible stench by wind directly into the entrails of their victims.[4]

Sixteenth-century naturalist and Spanish court physician Francisco Hernández (1514–1587), the author of *History of Animals of New Spain*, recounted claims that the flesh and dung of both the armadillo and the skunk (*izquiepatl*) offered cures for the dreaded

Thomas Bewick's rendering offers a more realistic illustration of the skunk as we know it, from Thomas Bewick, *A General History of Quadrupeds* (1790).

pox. South-of-the-border healing traditions include ingredients from skunk bodies and continue today in Mexico.[5] These practices will be discussed in more detail in chapter Four, 'Commodified Skunk'.

Recording his South American voyages, the English naturalist Charles Darwin (1809–1882) reported:

> We saw also a couple of Zorillos, or skunks, odious animals, which are far from uncommon. In general appearance the Zorillo resembles a polecat, but it is rather larger, and much thicker in proportion. Conscious of its power, it roams by day about the open plain, and fears neither dog nor man. If a dog is urged to the attack, its courage is instantly checked by a few drops of the fetid oil, which brings on violent sickness and running at the nose. Whatever is once polluted by it, is for ever useless. Azara says the smell can be perceived at a league distant; more than once, when entering the harbour of Monte Video, the wind being off shore, we have perceived the odour on board the *Beagle.* Certain it is, that every animal most willingly makes room for the Zorillo.[6]

Often confused with the New World skunk, the five-banded civet cat, pictured here on a stamp from Hong Kong, is an inexact term used for a variety of cat-like animals native to Africa and Asia.

Inconsistent naming can confuse; though *zorillo* and its variant spelling *zorilla* are often used interchangeably with 'skunk' in the work of Darwin and other early naturalists, they may also refer to a different species of stinky carnivorous mammal, *Ictonyx striatus*, which lives in Africa, also known as the 'African polecat', 'African skunk' or 'Cape polecat'. It seems most likely that the animal Darwin encountered was what Latin Americans typically call *zorillo*, meaning 'skunk', and more specifically in Darwin's case, Molina's hog-nosed skunk , to be discussed in chapter Three. Another variation on *zorillo/a* is *zorrino,* which may be more particular to parts of Argentina but shares the root 'zorro' for the

South American 'wolf-fox'. Uncertain terminologies and language differences, as well as assumptions made by Europeans classifying unfamiliar animals, may explain some of the confusion around animals who seemed, at first glance, to share certain phenotypic and morphological similarities.[7]

Skunks also found their way into the travel journals of Army Captain Meriwether Lewis (1774–1809) and his second-in-command, William Clark (1770–1838), as they led their Corps of Discovery expedition overland across the American West. Commissioned by President Thomas Jefferson, the Lewis and Clark expedition helped establish American sovereignty on 'uncharted' lands inhabited by Native peoples. Lewis and Clark documented dramatic discoveries of flora and fauna, including more than 200 plants and animals unknown to scientists at the time.

In addition to creating some of the first accurate maps of the Northwest, they chronicled in meticulous detail encounters with

The Patagonian hog-nosed skunk (*Conepatus humboldtii*), indigenous to Chile and Argentina.

members of more than 70 Indian nations, many of whom they characterized with the provinciality and hubris of those times. Thus members of the Sioux were deemed 'the vilest miscreants of the savage race', partly because the Sioux warred with other tribes, but also because they were not amenable to the intruding expedition, resisting practices like 'free trade' on the Missouri River. Despite harsh winter conditions and potentially fatal (on both sides) misunderstandings with Native peoples, Lewis and Clark persevered. Their writings about flora and fauna reflect excitement and the freshness of novelty. Legend elevates the role of Sacagawea, the famous Shoshone woman who, along with her French-Canadian fur-trapper husband Toussaint Charbonneau, accompanied Lewis and Clark to the Pacific Ocean. Reliable information is sketchy, but romanticized American lore records a brave and skilled Indian woman who acted as a friendly guide and interpreter, and whose

'Execution of the Inca' depicts the often-fatal conflicts between European invaders and indigenous peoples.

TURNING BEAR,
SIOUX WARRIOR.
COPYRIGHT 1900. J.A. ANDERSON

No. 900

A mural honours Sacagawea, the Shoshone guide, credited with escorting and translating for the European explorers Lewis and Clark on their expedition west.

reassuring presence made possible the successes of Lewis and Clark. The meaning of Sacagawea's name, sometimes translated as 'bird woman', and even the language of its origin, are uncertain. A plausible hypothesis is that *sacaga-wea* refers to a fur-bearing animal (after all, Charbonneau called his second Shoshone wife 'Otter Woman'). If so, *sacaga* might be a cognate of the Miami-Illinois *akaakwa* (related to the Abenaki *seganku*), signifying 'skunk', and thus Sacagawea would mean 'Skunk Woman'.

The skunk's place in the Lewis and Clark journals is not nearly as prominent as the romance of Sacagawea, but they first mention

A Sioux warrior, 1900, in Native dress, depicts what for many explorers was 'exotic' and 'dangerous'.

23

This *Mephitis mephitis* and relations engraving, from *Illustrations of Zoology* (1851), drawn according to Georges Cuvier, furthered mistaken assumptions about the skunk's evolutionary connections.

'polecats' in 1805 just after the expedition crossed the Missouri River. In 1806 Lewis offers a fuller description of the striped skunk:

> The Pole-cat is also found in every part of the country. They are very abundant on some parts of the Columbia, particularly in the neighbourhood of the great falls and narrows of that river, where the[y] live in the clifts along the river and feed on the offal of the Indian fishing shores. These are the same as those of other parts of North America.[8]

The striped skunk's Linnaean name derives from the Latin word *mephitis*, or 'bad odour'. The genus *Mephitis* was established in 1795 by the French naturalist Georges Cuvier (1769–1832).[9] In his encyclopedia of quadrupeds of 1777, German naturalist Johann C. D. von Schreber (1739–1810) introduced the name *Mephitis mephitis* at the species level, and was also one of the first scientists to describe the skunk anatomically. However, it appears that Schreber's descriptions were founded not on direct observations, but on the work of the French naturalist Georges-Louis Leclerc, Comte de Buffon (1707–1788). This might have been fine except that Buffon, in turn, likely based his descriptions of the *zorillo* (he did not use Linnaean nomenclature) on two specimens belonging to a Parisian curate, M. Aubrey, and did not consider traveller accounts as some of his predecessors had. Buffon mistakenly believed the animals were either Peruvian or from some other region of the Spanish possessions, misinformation that Schreber apparently depended on. Eager to correct Buffon's error, American zoologist Arthur Holmes Howell (1872–1940) speculated that the skunks in question more likely belonged to a species he believed hailed from Florida or Mexico.[10]

But American ornithologist and zoologist Joel Asaph Allen (1838–1921) concluded that neither specimen was from the U.S. Further problems with nomenclature and the questionable geographic origins of the animals only heightened the confusion. Allen proposed that the error was made because '"le cinche" and "le zorille" were described and figured from poorly stuffed skins' in Aubrey's cabinet and became convinced that Schreber's *Viverra mephitis* was actually 'a compound of the Mexican Coatis and Mexican Skunks, and . . . not citable as a term entitled to consideration in nomenclature'.[11]

Challenging Howell's 'radical changes . . . made in the nomenclature of the North American skunks', Allen viewed it as his duty

to expose Howell's regrettable alterations in the generic names of *Mephitis* and *Spilogale*.[12] According to Allen's impassioned analysis, Howell's revisions of the skunk in the genus *Mephitis* constituted important and accurate work, but Allen roundly differed with Howell in the cases of *Mephitis mephitica* (Shaw) and *Mephitis putida* (Boitard).[13]

Some of the confusion may have evolved from another error made a century and a half earlier by the English naturalist Mark Catesby (1682–1749). Catesby spent much of his life in the United States and is best known for authoring the first publication devoted to North American plants and animals, replete with the first colour folio-sized plates to be found in a work of natural history. Catesby's work offers an illuminating glimpse into the heightened Enlightenment interest in science and the natural world.

Mark Catesby's famous polecat drawing, which caused a lot of trouble, from *The Natural History of Carolina, Florida and the Bahama Islands* (1754).

'Le Cinche' from Georges-Louis Leclerc, *Histoire naturelle* (1749–1804). Leclerc had never actually seen a live skunk.

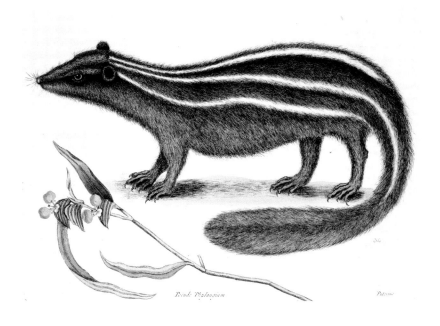

Putois Phalangium   *Putois*

Fig. 1. *Japanischer Dachs* [Meles Anakuma.] Fig. 2. *Teledu* [Mydaus meliceps.] Fig. 3. *Honig Ratel* [Ratelus capensis.]
Fig. 4. *Spitzfrett* [Helictis orientalis.] Fig. 5. *Stinkthier* [Mephitis suffocans.] Fig. 6. *Vielfrass* [Gulo borealis.]

Common striped skunk (*Mephitis mephitis*), drawing from Edward W. Nelson, *Wild Animals of North America* (1918).

Another example of erronenous connections between the skunk family and weasels, badgers and civet cats, from Ferdinand Krauss, *Die Säugethiere nach Familien und Gattungen* (1851).

But Allen was convinced that Catesby's inaccurate drawing and description of *Putorius americanus striatus* led astray a number of scientific successors, including Linnaeus. Allen chose to 'take the most charitable view of the case', calling Catesby's drawing 'a confused recollection of the little spotted skunk and the common skunk, and not on any animal he ever met in nature'.[14]

In 1845 French biologist Charles-Lucien (Carlo) Jules Laurent Bonaparte, with his own illustrious family tree, may have been the first to recognize that skunks were morphologically exceptional. Though he did not further explain and may not have even understood why exactly the skunk was different, he made a significant contribution to classifying skunks at the family level as Mephitidae (he called them *Mephitina*). What might now be viewed as an insightful designation from the nineteenth century would lay the foundation for reclassifying skunks in the twenty-first.

This brief history illustrates that it is no easy matter to determine who gets to be a skunk and how, and why. The story of skunk taxonomy reminds us that the particular cultures and worldviews of individual scientists in the context of their times affect the way animals are perceived, understood and categorized.

As independent development of similar traits like molars and enlarged scent glands found in skunks and weasels demonstrates, anatomy, it turns out, is not always evolutionary destiny. Anatomical similarities can suggest misleading hypotheses of evolutionary relationships. Consider the long-standing controversy among zoologists, challenged by new evidence, that the hippopotamus, despite greater obvious structural resemblance to the pig, actually shares much closer common ancestry with the whale.[15] It is possible that in the future, much like the shift in the hippo-whale-pig debate, new hypotheses and evidence about the skunk's pedigree may be unearthed, resulting in another kaleidoscopic round of taxonomic shift.

In the skilled hands of diligent researchers, newer techniques of inquiry offer fresh understandings of how skunks fit into the evolving tree of life. Jerry Dragoo's work on skunk evolution and his remarkable findings and theories that skunks are not of the weasel family are especially worthy of praise.

2 Skunks in Not So Black and White

As explorer Meriwether Lewis correctly noted, the skunk is a ubiquitous figure throughout North America, with skunks also ranging south through Mexico and into Central and South America.

Skunks in the Americas are most readily identified by the conspicuous black-and-white patterns of their glossy coats and generous, feathery tails, but not all skunks come in black and white. Some display pelages of brown, grey or creamy hues. Though many striped skunks appear to be predominantly either black or white, the latter are not albinos. Albino skunks are rare and unlikely to survive in the wild, given their weakened immune systems and lack of warning coloration, leaving them susceptible to predators.

Markings are typified by stripes or spots, the latter actually a series of interrupted stripes. Some may also sport white blazes on the nose, or white hoods, or both. Those selectively bred in captivity flaunt numerous colour variations not seen in the wild.

In build, skunks are thicker-bodied than weasels but less stocky than badgers. With its delicate, triangular-shaped head, and small, bright eyes, a skunk might, at first glance, be mistaken for a cat. However, the rolling gait, or 'waddle', quickly distinguishes skunks from their feline counterparts. Skunks are plantigrade, meaning they walk the way we humans do, with the full sole of

MEPHITIS CHILENSIS.
Mus. Paris.
Native of S. America.

Mephitis chilensis, a brown-hued skunk naturally found in the wild, from Charles Hamilton Smith, *Mammalia,* vol. xv, in William Jardine, ed., *The Naturalist's Library* (1845–6).

the foot flat on the ground. Other plantigrade mammals include raccoons, possums, bears, rabbits, rats and mice, hedgehogs and kangaroos, whereas dogs, cats and birds, for example, are digitigrade, walking on their toes.

Skunks vary in weight from just 450 kg (1 lb) (spotted skunk) to a hefty 7 kg (15 lb) (striped skunk) or 8 kg (18 lb) (hog-nosed skunk), placing the size of a skunk somewhere between that of the weasel and the badger, both of whom are members of the family Mustelidae. The skunk's earlier scientific grouping within the mustelid family was erroneously based, in part, on similar tooth morphology that distinguished skunks and mustelids from other carnivores. But as scientists began to suspect, tooth morphology alone does not a mustelid make. And neither do the enlarged anal glands with which the skunk in particular is so generously endowed. Secrets that initially eluded scientists about the skunk are now emerging from the shadows; the history of skunk taxonomy offers an intriguing tale in its own right.

Classified as mammals, skunks belong to the order Carnivora, which included, as of 45 million years ago, four of what are now recognized as modern families: civets (Viverridae), cats (Felidae), wolves (Canidae) and weasels (Mustelidae). Today, more than a dozen Carnivora families are generally acknowledged by taxonomists, including families as diverse as bear (Ursidae), mongoose (Herpestidae), hyena (Hyaenidae), seal (Phocidae), walrus (Odobenidae) and raccoon (Procyonidae).

Though long grouped with badgers, weasels and martens, skunks are now believed to deserve their very own family, Mephitidae, which, like the genus and species names for the striped skunk, *Mephitis mephitis*, translates to 'stink'. Reliance by earlier scientists on tooth morphologies (what was once a second

These albino baby skunks, Rita and Jake, are the product of selective, domestic breeding for pets.

The trail of the common skunk, from Nelson, *Wild Animals of North America*, shows both the plantigrade walking pattern and the dexterous hand-like front paw.

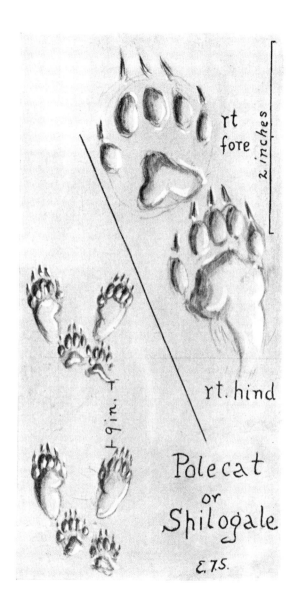

rt fore

2 inches

rt. hind

Polecat
or
Spilogale

E. T. S.

9 in.

The skeleton of a hog-nosed skunk (*Conepatus* spp.) with digging claws, on display at the Museum of Osteology in Oklahoma City.

molar on the upper jaw, and the lack of a carnassial notch on the upper fourth pre-molar), and enlarged scent glands of both skunks and weasels, led them to assume the two animals were mono-phyletic. However, the skunk's highly developed scent glands are nipple-shaped and spray with hose-like precision, differentiating them from the anal ducts of mustelids. Many scientists are now convinced that these shared characteristics exemplify 'convergent evolution', whereby comparable traits develop independently in unrelated or peripherally related organisms. Separate ancestry was suspected as early as the mid-nineteenth century, but scientists were only more recently able to confirm it, with the help of mito-chondrial DNA and fossil record evidence.[1] The skunk provides a good example of the 'squishiness' of human efforts to classify animals.

While scientists had generally recognized twelve species of skunks (with some sources counting thirteen), a more recent and

Franz Kruger's illustration of *Mephitis suffocans*, and *M. zorilla*, with details of skunk skull and dentition, from Hinrich Lichtenstein, *Darstellung neuer und wenig bekannter Säugethiere in Abbildungen und Beschreibungen* (Berlin, 1827–34).

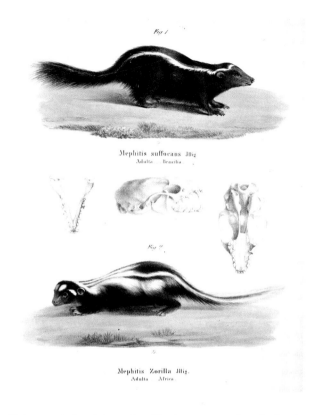

Fig /

Mephitis suffocans Illig
Adulta   Brasilia

Fig 2.

Mephitis Zorilla Illig.
Adulta   Africa

widely accepted update on classification synonymizes the South American hog-nosed skunk (also known as the Patagonian skunk) with Molina's skunk and thus reduces the total by one species.[2]

Despite some disagreement, most sources now cite three New World skunk genera (*Conepatus*, *Mephitis* and *Spilogale*), as well as a fourth, the Asian stink badger (*Mydaus*). And though they live an ocean away, Asian stink badgers were originally grouped with skunks, then taxonomically relocated to join badgers, and more recently returned to the skunk family.

As skunk nomenclature and classification were hotly debated by experts, skunks managed to weasel out of easy categorization.

While taxonomy is not etched in stone, it is still useful to adopt the reasonably consistent division of skunks into four currently recognized genera: *Mephitis*, *Spilogale*, *Conepatus* and *Mydaus*.[3]

The prototypical skunk image for North American residents is the striped skunk (*Mephitis mephitis*). The reduplicated Latin root can be translated as 'stinky, stinky'. With black coats, and patterns of white stripes on the back, head and tail, this species is the version of skunk most commonly represented in visual culture.

The striped skunk's range extends throughout southern Canada, the u.s. and northern Mexico. Diverse though not obligate (restricted) carnivores that operate as omnivores, striped skunks are mostly opportunistic eaters. A skunk's diet typically consists of plant materials, grubs and insects and the occasional bird egg. Because they also eat creatures that humans consider nuisances, like rodents and insect larvae harmful to crops and gardens,

Franz Kruger's illustration of *Mephitis mesomelas*, from Lichtenstein's *Darstellung neuer und wenig bekannter Säugethiere in Abbildungen und Beschreibungen.*

Fig. 2.

skunks make handy neighbours and play important roles in the ecosystem. Though known for the occasional raid on chicken coops, they share another gustatory penchant with bears and raccoons – namely, the honey bee – with the skunk considered by some beekeepers to be a strong contender for the title of most offending predator. Apiaries offer high-protein smorgasbords for skunks who know exactly how to trick guard bees by cleverly scratching at the entrance of the hive to lure them out. When guard bees emerge, the skunks snag them with their front paws and roll them along the ground to minimize the chance of being stung. Even if stung, skunks seem relatively unfazed. As oblivious worker bees stream out, the skunks settle down for a delectable and leisurely meal. Given their methodical patience, a family of hungry skunks can do significant colony damage in a night's work. As long as there are still bees to be consumed, it's not uncommon for them to return repeatedly, and if they gain access to the hive itself, skunks may finish with a delicious dessert of honey and wax. Evidence of skunks includes scratched earth, bare ground or holes around the apiary, and lumps of leftover hive residents. But beekeepers can significantly discourage the nocturnal poachers by elevating or screening the hive door. While skunks' appetites for beehives pose a nuisance, the scale of skunk hive mischief is negligible compared to the colony collapse crisis in North America and Europe caused by parasitic mites, mass collateral deaths from pesticides, loss of meadow habitat and commercial apiculture methods. Of benefit to humans is the skunks' partiality for yellow-jacket nests, particularly when cooler autumn weather brings the seasonal delicacy of larvae they so relish. While digging yellow jackets out of the ground, skunks helpfully destroy nests as they go.

Though their preferred habitat is wooded areas and fields, skunks readily adapt to suburban and urban neighbourhoods, where buildings, culverts, rubbish, lawns and gardens offer ready food and shelter. Skunks will dig their own underground dens, but are just as likely to assume ownership of dens deserted by other burrowing animals. The striped skunk's warning coloration deters most ground predators, which have evolved to recognize potential trouble in the variations on the single thick stripe of white across the back and tail. But skunks have a harder time shaking persistent aerial predators like the great horned owl, which can swiftly perform a sneak attack from above and doesn't give a hoot about catching a blast of spray.

Rarer and more secretive cousins are hooded skunks, *Mephitis macroura*, so named for the fancy white ruff encircling their necks. Their pelage typically grows in three colour patterns: black with a fully white back, black with two thin white stripes, or the less common combination thereof. The Greek *macroura* is an etymological nod to their disproportionately 'long tails' – their body length is only about 30 cm (1 ft) and their weight about 900 g (2 lb). Hooded skunks once ranged in the south-western United States, and while less common there, are still plentiful in Mexico. Though they will set up house in desert and rocky canyons, they prefer grassy stream areas. Mostly vegetarian, hooded skunks have a particular proclivity for prickly pear, but their diet also includes insects, small vertebrates and bird eggs.

Hog-nosed skunks (*Conepatus*), so named for their elongated noses with naked pads resembling pig snouts, are generally black with a large band of white on the backside and a white bushy tail. The genus *Conepatus* had long been divided into four species, until a recent scientific consensus found reason to treat Molina's hog-nosed skunk, *Conepatus chinga*, and Humboldt's (or Patagonian) hog-nosed skunk, *Conepatus humboldti*, as one, reducing the number of species in *Conepatus* from four to three.

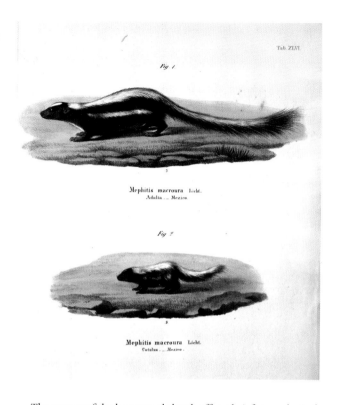

Tab. XLVI.

Fig 1

Mephitis macroura Licht.
Adulta. — Mexico.

Fig 2

Mephitis macroura Licht.
Catulus. — Mexico.

The names of the hog-nosed skunk offer a brief etymological detour highlighting regional and cultural themes. Those familiar with Spanish may puzzle over 'chinga', the second name for Molina's skunk and a word most often associated with an offensive vulgarity, particularly in Mexico. However, *chinga* in parts of Argentina can be used quite innocently as an adjective for 'little' or 'short'.[4] 'Chinga' as a noun was alternatively hypothesized to have possible connections to a geographical name, as the Chingas District in a Peruvian province might suggest. But Juan Ignacio Molina (1740–1829) himself, who is credited with the nomenclature, was relying on an indigenous word for skunk, *chinghue* (*viverra chinga*) or *El Chingue*. The word comes from the language of the Mapuche, one of a diverse group of indigenous people in south-central Chile and the Argentinian west whose language was called 'Araucanian' by the Spanish colonizers.[5]

Among Argentinians, the South American hog-nosed skunk is commonly referred to as 'zorrino'. However, in the northeastern part of the country and regions of Paraguay, the indigenous Guanari language offers up *Yagua-né*, which translates as 'stinking [*né*] dog [*yaguá*]'.

The genus name *Conepatus* derives from *conepatl*, which translates as 'little fox' in an indigenous language of Mexico. The prefix *cone* means 'young' or 'child'. *Epatl* is the word for 'fox', assigned

A drawing of Humboldt's hog-nosed skunk, now synonymous with Molina's skunk.

by naturalist J. E. Gray in the nineteenth century. The hog-nosed skunk was historically divided into two species: the Eastern *Conepatus leuconotus* and Western *Conepatus mesoleucus*, which have now been merged under the title American hog-nosed skunk, or sometimes white-backed hog-nosed skunk.

What follows is a quick look at each of the three currently recognized species of hog-nosed skunks.

The range of *Conepatus leuconotus*, the American hog-nosed skunk, extends from northern Nicaragua through central Guatemala and Honduras to Mexico (though this species is not found on the Baja Peninsula). Although American hog-nosed skunks were once also present in the southeastern part of Texas, southern Arizona and southern New Mexico, they are disappearing from the u.s. While hog-nosed skunks are not yet designated as 'Vulnerable', their populations are dwindling and their status deserves to be revisited in the near future. A number of factors are suspected in their declining numbers: human agricultural and development practices result in deforestation and fragmentation, thereby destroying habitat; and the use of pesticides and livestock overgrazing also make affected lands less hospitable to these skunks. Deaths by motor vehicles are numerous, not to mention, to a lesser extent, encounters with feral hogs and territorial disputes with striped skunks.

A single white stripe starts at the American hog-nosed skunk's forehead, broadens at the shoulders and extends to the back of the tail, which is almost completely white. Its typical habitat includes canyons, streams and desert scrub. Known in Texas as 'the rooter skunk', the hog-nosed skunk will eat small rodents but prefers insects, grubs, larvae and vegetation. The forearms of hog-nosed skunks are particularly strong, making them competent climbers, though they lack the agility of smaller spotted skunks. While also equipped with the smelly defence, hog-nosed skunks prefer to stay out of sight. If pursued, hog-nosed skunks may rise up on their hind legs and sometimes even walk forwards before dropping back to the ground. Hog-nosed skunks are also known to hiss at predators, and even send dirt flying backwards by paddling their front paws. When frightened and in defence mode, they may crouch down, stomp and raise their tails before sending aggressive predators flat on their backs. If scare tactics and bared teeth don't work, the hog-nosed skunk will proceed to bite or spray the predator, or both.

Commonly known as the striped hog-nosed, or Amazonian hog-nosed, *Conepatus semistriatus* is considered neotropical. Though described by some as an 'edge species' – a term some assign to animals who make borders and fringes of forest lands their habitats – far-ranging striped hog-nosed skunks can be found from southern Mexico all the way into northern Peru along the western Andes and into eastern Venezuela and Los Llanos of Colombia, with some inhabiting eastern Brazil. Depending on the time of year, hog-nosed skunks will migrate from deciduous forests and grasslands during the dry season to higher elevations during the rainy season, presumably driven by their quest for food, which includes birds, lizards and insects. Relatively adaptable to disruptions by humankind, they are not yet considered endangered, though their populations have been adversely affected by commercial hunting for their pelts.

Like their other hog-nosed relatives, the populations of Molina's hog-nosed skunks are also decreasing, though not yet drastically enough to be placed on the endangered lists of global conservation agencies like the International Union for Conservation of Nature (IUCN), World Wildlife Fund (WWF) and Convention on International Trade in Endangered Species of Wild Fauna and Flora (CITES). Found from the middle to the southern tip of South America, they are considered native to

Argentina, Bolivia, Chile, Paraguay, Peru and Uruguay. But the secretive nature of Molina's skunks makes for a thinner understanding of their ecological lifestyle, adding an element of mystery. It is speculated that they prefer arid climes and open savannahs where they can forage in private for eggs, beetles, birds and small mammals, though when they are not busy feeding, they retreat to enclosed, shrubby and rocky areas. Overgrazing in Patagonia by animals used for the meat industry, combined with substantial hunting of skunks for their fur in the 1970s and '80s, deleteriously affected their populations.

Fossil research suggests that the spotted skunk, a member of the genus *Spilogale*, is more primal than either *Mephitis* or *Conepatus*, and also more cat-like. Typically black, the beautiful silky coat is punctuated with four to six broken white stripes resembling spots. *Spilogale* skunks climb trees and make dens in crevices or burrows, sometimes under buildings. Approximately 40 cm (16 in.) long and weighing 450 g (1 lb), they are seen across the u.s. and Mexico. They fall into four species: Western spotted (*Spilogale gracilis*), Eastern spotted (*Spilogale putorius*), Southern spotted (*Spilogale angustifrons*) and pygmy spotted (*Spilogale pygmaea*). Pygmy skunks are the only members of Mephitidae that have been classified as 'Vulnerable', according to the iucn Red List. A booming Pacific Coast tourist industry and the construction of roads and resorts have contributed to reducing their population by a hefty one-third.

The Western spotted skunk, *Spilogale gracilis,* sports a pattern of interrupted white stripes on a sleek black coat, with the flourish of a white-tipped tail. Ranging throughout the American West, as far north as British Columbia and as far south as Central America, Western skunks are smaller and speedier, and more carnivorous than their striped counterparts. Dietary preferences include mice, crickets, caterpillars, birds, lizards and carrion.

While bobcats, foxes, coyotes and dogs pose threats, their primary predator is the great horned owl.

Though primarily insectivores, Eastern spotted skunks, *Spilogale putorius*, are excellent mousers. Fond of bird eggs, they will use their front paws to lob an egg back through their hind legs to crack the shell. In addition to their impressive spotted coats, they are famous for the remarkable handstand they resort to when confronted by an enemy. Eastern spotted skunks are readily distinguished from their Western counterparts by a smaller white spot between the eyes, narrower stripes on their backs and sides, and tails tipped with tufts of white hair. Because they consume crop-damaging insects and rodents, they are good for agriculture. Populations of both Eastern and Western spotted

The island spotted skunk (*Spilogale gracilis amphiala*) tends to be smaller than her striped counterpart, and sports a beautiful, dramatic coat that has been used in the fur industry for coats and capes.

skunks are decreasing, though the decline cannot be blamed on hunting. Instead, motor vehicle road deaths and pest control management efforts like poisoning and trapping have taken their toll.

Technically an Old World animal, the extraordinary looking stink badger (perhaps deserving a name change!) shares with her New World cousins similar characteristics in teeth, brain and middle ear, along with the infamous defence. Physically, the stink badger resembles a cryptozoological hybrid of mole, badger and possum. The word *Mydaus* derives from a Greek word that approximates 'damp' and 'decay', offering a nod to the smell. Two species of stink badger can be found, respectively, on the western side of the Malaysian archipelago and on the Philippine island of Palawan. The Sunda (or Teledu, *M. javanensis*) is native to Indonesia and Malaysia; the Palawan stink badger (*M. marchei*) lives in the Philippines and is classified as 'Vulnerable'. The Palawan stink badger is mostly brown or black, with a sprinkling of white hairs. Palawan stink badgers move with an awkward gait, and their approach to self-defence has its own peculiar twist. If snarling and teeth-baring aren't effective, they may 'play possum' (pretending to be dead), turning their hind ends towards attackers in warning.

Once erroneously assumed to be related to the common badger, stink badgers were reclassified into the family of Mephitidae, as recent DNA evidence points to common ancestry with skunks. This reassignment of the stink badgers of Indonesia and the Philippines to the clade of Mephitidae coincides with hypotheses that ancient ancestors of Mephitidae made their way across Beringia, on the Bering land bridge between what are now Siberia and Alaska. The discovery of a perfectly preserved skull and lower jaw of the *Martinogale faull* ancestral skunk in 1974, also known as the Red Rock Canyon (California) skunk, supports

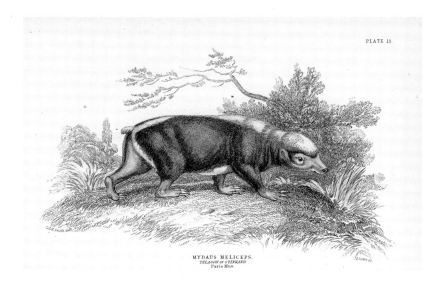

PLATE 15.

MYDAUS MELICEPS.
TELAGON or STINKARD.
Paris Mus.

claims of a prehistoric migration from the Old World to the New that would have taken place more than 9 million years ago.[6] Though similar in size to American skunks, falling somewhere between the striped and spotted varieties, stink badgers lack the eye-catching beauty of their New World cousins.

A mid-19th-century engraving of a stink badger (*Mydaus javanensis*).

Most skunks are skilled diggers, equipped with long front claws to unearth burrows for nesting, and excavate grubs and rodents for food. Though nearsighted (or short-sighted), with poor vision, skunks are furnished with a terrific sense of smell, even if they don't always 'smell good'. They also have excellent hearing and finely tuned senses of touch and taste.

In the wild, skunks are nocturnal (some would argue 'crepuscular') foragers who easily adapt to various environments that include mountains, deserts and forests. As human development encroaches on habitat, they have adapted to both urban and suburban areas, where many human denizens have

An intact skunk
skull.

come to view them as pests. Though most skunk species are not
currently endangered, proximity to humans and road traffic
increases the dangers they face.

Mating, gestation and communal denning habits vary across
skunk species. Though most mate once a year, timing can fluctuate
over several months in winter. Exceptions to this are the mating
patterns of Western spotted skunks and pygmy skunks, which
typically mate in late summer or early autumn, but with
implantation delayed until March or April, so that the young are
born in May. Delaying egg implantation after fertilization is a
remarkable characteristic found in a number of other mammal
species, too, including grizzly bears. This seasonal delay strategy
evidently allows females to access the choicest potential mates in
the late summer, and times birth-giving for the more optimal
warmer months. Whenever and however it happens, skunk mating
is almost always a redolent occasion. As a general practice, skunks
don't spray other skunks, but females may spray males they are
rejecting, and males may spray other males in a bid for a female's

attention. True to their independent natures, skunks are polygamous and do not form enduring romantic relationships. Once mating season is over, and male skunks have made their genetic contribution, they absent themselves from parenting duties.

Baby skunks, called either kittens or kits, are born sightless and hairless, and completely dependent on their mothers. Litters typically produce four to eight offspring, but litter size may vary between as few as two and as many as a dozen. The particular colour patterns of what will become their fur are already faintly outlined on the kits' hairless skin. Born with functioning scent glands, they typically do not spray, though when their eyes open between two and four weeks, they may self-defend if startled. Kits are curious and playful and love to wrestle and tumble under the watchful eyes of their mothers. Mother skunks are characteristically devoted, keeping kits close by for the first six months while teaching them the skills for surviving on their own.

Engraving of Stinkdas (*Mydaus meliceps*), or 'stink badger'; this species is now classified as *Mydaus javanensis* and is unrelated to the badger.

Skunks readily communicate through body language and vocalizations that may include attention-seeking bird-like chirps, whimpers and grunts when frightened or upset, or 'lip smacking', a sign of contentment. They also often express a range of emotions and sensations such as anger, pain, curiosity and the desire to play. Often a foraging skunk will utter snuffling sounds while burrowing through underbrush. During the winter, skunks do not technically hibernate, but in cold climates, skunks, like bears, may go into a temporary dormancy called a 'state of torpor', remaining in their dens for periods of time and relying on stored body fat. During this time, their metabolism and oxygen intake decelerate. Sleep may be intermittently interrupted by brief bouts of wakefulness, and if weather appeals, a skunk will leave its den. While some skunks prefer to den alone, when they emerge in early spring, they lack the body fat of those who denned communally. Female skunks typically inhabit a communal den, and occasionally a male will join them for warmth.

Though skunks are not native to the United Kingdom, reports of a colony of wild skunks in the Forest of Dean, Gloucestershire, made headlines in 2009. Treated sceptically at first, these sightings were eventually verified and followed by other reports of skunks on the loose. This raised speculation that skunks might have a previously unknown native connection to the British Isles. A more probable explanation is that these skunks were originally raised as pets but abandoned by breeders after the UK made it illegal in 2007 to remove the animals' stink glands.

3 Essence of Skunk

Cutting straight to the source of the skunk's 'bad rap', we encounter what Ernest Thompson Seton dubbed 'the smell gun', the animal's specially developed anal scent glands that produce the distinctive, sulphurous spray.[1]

Charles Darwin disparaged the 'odious animals' that emit a 'fetid oil' that brings on violent sickness and runny noses.[2] His open distaste for the skunk is echoed by other Europeans making their first encounters. Juan Ignacio Molina (1740–1829), the Chilean Jesuit priest and naturalist credited with naming the hog-nosed skunk, denounces skunk spray as 'disgusting to every other animal':

> [it] proceeds from a greenish oil contained in a vesicle placed, as in the pole-cat, near the anus. When the animal is attacked, it elevates its posteriors and scatters the loathsome liquid upon its assailant. Nothing can equal the offensiveness of its smell; it penetrates everywhere, and may be perceived at a great distance. Garments that are infected with it cannot be worn for a long time and not until repeated washings; and the dogs, after having been engaged with the *chinghue*, run to the water, roll themselves in the mud, howl as if they were mad, and will eat nothing as long as the smell continues about them.[3]

The smell of skunk spray has been characterized variously as rotten eggs, burning rubber or plastic, natural gas, old garlic, dirty dog and onions. Low concentrations of the redolent repellant, emitted up close or in passing, are sufficient to grab the attention of even the casually assailed. Skunk spray consists of sulphur-based compounds that differ from those found in garlic, and are readily detected by human noses at the tiniest of levels. But not everyone finds skunk smell repugnant. The spectrum includes those who are relatively oblivious to even high concentrations, while other people respond with ecstatic delight.

In point of fact, skunk smell has a long, if not esoteric, connection to things sensual and sexual. Like other rich animal scents, it has even been enjoyed as an aphrodisiac. Researchers studying the olfactory sense and sexual arousal found evidence of a significant connection; smell is an important factor in sexual stimulation and plays a subtle role in choosing a mate. The 'chemistry' of desire between romantic partners appears to have strong biological roots. It may well be that the 'soul mate' who so compellingly inspires our loftiest sentiments really just smells good! The long connection between fragrance and sexual arousal is nowhere more evident than in the perfume industry. Musk taken from animals like civet, muskrat and skunk became an important base in perfume to help convey its scent.

The well-known Chanel No. 5 illustrates the inherent paradox of combining the fetid with the fragrant to create pleasing and Eros-inducing scents. American essayist Diane Ackerman describes the various aromatic layers:

Its top note – the one you smell first – is the aldehyde, then your nose detects the middle note of jasmine, lily of the valley . . . and finally, the base note, which carries the perfume and makes it linger . . . Base notes are almost always of animal origin, ancient emissaries of smell that transport us across woodlands and savannas.[4]

Top notes offering the first impression of a scent are typically light and volatile, and evaporate quickly. Middle notes, also known as 'heart notes', surface more gradually in the dispersion process and are typically imbued with flowery or fruity aromas. Base notes are heavier, depicted as 'mammalian sex attractants with a distinctly urinous or faecal odour', and combine with the middle notes to create the body of the perfume.[5] Musk was traditionally derived from plant and animal sources, the latter involving prolonged suffering and ultimately the death of the animal. But increased costs and more recent concern for animal welfare prompted a move towards the predominant use of

A dramatic view of the back end of a beautiful white skunk, Nemo, who, fortunately for readers, is not actually 'fully loaded'.

The skunk anal scent sac after removal.

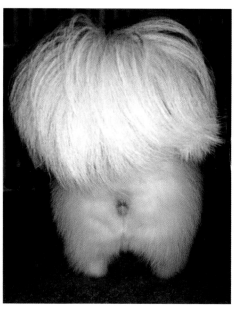

This 'Howdy from a Little Stinker' postcard offers a familiar, if affectionate, take on the skunk's distinctive odour.

synthetics in perfume manufacturing, even though use of animal-derived sources continues.

The olfactory ambivalences many humans experience towards corporeal smells may reflect the ambiguity felt towards our own animality. The desire to distance ourselves from the natural body is evidenced in the popularity of scented soaps and deodorants, deemed essential in certain cultures to modern personal hygiene. But even in ancient cultures like Egypt, China, India, Greece and Rome, rituals and traditions modified natural body odour through the application of various natural fragrances and scents, including honey and extracts of flowers and herbs. Over time, perfumes proved to have utilitarian as well as aesthetic advantages to cover up smells associated with disease and even death. In Western culture, while fragrances and essential oils were often put to medicinal uses, they were equally useful in abating offensive body odour, particularly during the medieval era when public bathing was eventually condemned by the Church. Commercial fragrances rose in popularity among the upper classes wishing to smell good, but remained unaffordable for anyone else, creating a gap between the powdered and perfumed elite, and the unwashed masses.

When perfume manufacturing shifted to the use of synthetics in the nineteenth century, it placed commercial fragrance within easier financial reach of the masses.

Associations with the bestial and the primitive also contributed to anxiety about body odour. Real-life human prejudices are often articulated in the rhetoric of 'dirty' or 'smelly'. French prostitutes are known as *putains*, a word deriving from a Latin root meaning 'stinking'. Good smells are often associated with virtue and higher social status, and smelling 'bad' with disease, wrongdoing and the lower classes, notions that still persist today. Whether the distinctions are based on socio-economic, cultural or racial differences, the strategy of 'othering' enables one group to distance itself from another. Thus the intensity and power of skunk musk, and the strong reactions it produces, offer a chance to examine our feelings about bodily smells of both humans and non-human animals. The contemporary American obsession with 'body odour' and masking smells, in particular, stems from an anxiety fed, and capitalized on, by advertisers hawking products from scented laundry soaps to deodorants for our bodies, houses and cars. In the U.S. alone, the perfume and fragrance industry is a $5 billion retail business. But natural scents and oils have also long been important to traditional religious and spiritual rituals across numerous cultures, and in some cases adorning the body in fragrance was thought to bring one closer to the divine.

Of the five senses, the olfactory continues to be the least valued in contemporary Western culture, despite direct connections between smell and pleasures, taste, emotion and memory. Starting with Plato's ancient disparagement of the sense of smell and the privileging of sight by various Western philosophers, smell was relegated to the lowest ranks. This human disaffection for the sense of smell is likely also another brick in the ideological wall erected between humans and animals, since for many animals, like the skunk, the nose is a richly developed instrument for perceiving and interpreting the world, often more valuable than sight.

And yet, according to some scientists, the sense of smell is more than important. Human noses, to varying degrees, are specifically attuned to musky scents, the effects of which, in the case of, say, the scent of musk deer, may resemble testosterone. Used as an aphrodisiac from early civilizations in Asia until today, animal musk has had a long tradition of enhancing sexual desire. Ted Andrews, who writes about the spiritual and magical powers of animals, also explores the connection between sexual response and fragrance, citing scientific 'work with pheromones and studies that reveal surprising similarity between the cells of and response of the olfactory nerves, and those within the genitalia'. Particularly for those for whom skunks are a totem animal, the appearance of a skunk, Andrews asserts, may generate strong sexual responses, along with a renewed ability to attract others.[6]

In the novel *Chérie*, French writer Edmond de Goncourt describes the secret pleasures of animal musk when his title character discovers that by inhaling the scent of 'un grain de musc du Thibet' she can bring herself to orgasm.[7] Animal musk has a global history as a sexual stimulant, celebrated in various literatures, particularly in Asia and Europe, for its power to trigger sexual ecstasy. Victorian sex researcher Havelock Ellis devoted a number of pages to the effects and uses of animal musk, which he claimed could lead to swoons and even manias, particularly in women. In real life, it served as a cure for women's 'sexual torpor'. Europe's predilection for musk developed after it was discovered via Persia as 'the most cherished perfume of the Islamic world', though its popularity diminished as musk became associated with the less refined and more primitive self.[8] Like other animals, humans have olfactory receptors to which odour

Charles M. Russell, *Man's Weapons Are Useless When Nature Goes Armed (Weapons of the Weak; Two of a Kind Win)*, oil on canvas, 1916, depicts the full power of the skunk.

molecules bind, but scientists don't really know yet exactly how olfactory receptors work. Olfactory responses are deeply personal, meaning that not all people react the same way to the same odours. How we experience smell depends on the chemistry of the odour molecules, as well as the genetic predisposition of the human.[9]

Cultural anxieties and discomforts surrounding bodily odours and functions like sex often find release in humour. The popular sex-obsessed and stinky cartoon skunk Pepé Le Pew offers a perfect example. Ardently persistent despite the cloud of *odeur fetide* trailing him, Pepé continues his relentless quest for *amour*, proclaiming, 'I am ze locksmith of love, no?'[10] As Ackerman explains, scent gland secretions from animals like deer, boar and cats, among others, 'assume the same chemical shape as a steroid, and when we smell them we may respond as we would to human pheromones'.[11] Pheromones are chemical or hormonal substances that, when secreted, trigger physiological and behavioural responses (including sexual response) in other organisms. The effect of pheromones on human sexual attraction and mating patterns is less clear, though subtle smell cues may well be at work in mate selection.[12]

Skunk musk is stored in two glands, one on either exterior side of the skunk's anal opening, each connected to a papilla, a small nipple-like projection. So effective is this weapon of self-defence that it permits the skunk the muscular control to take aim and fire with great precision. Against predators within view, the skunk can specifically target their faces. For unseen predators in hot pursuit, the skunk can cut loose with a more generalized wave of spray that will likely bring the chase to a screeching halt. It is easy to speculate that the human fear of misting skunk spray finds some correspondence with an old belief that diseases were caused by 'bad air'.

Known as Miasma Theory, with roots extending back to ancient times around the globe, the notion that a bad smell or offensive odours were disease persisted well into the mid-nineteenth century until germ theory and the role of bacteria emerged to explain epidemics like cholera and typhoid, and diseases like dysentery and influenza. That skunk musk is known to be irritating to the eyes and may even cause temporary blindness on contact helps to explain some of the hyperbolic theories asserting that skunk spray can permanently maim or kill its victims.

The backside anatomy of the striped skunk offers a particular example of unique evolution, as the skunk is the only animal to have perfected this musky defence into a sharply honed skill. Skunks are usually equipped with a sufficient store for half a dozen shots at a time. Various sources opine that it can take skunks anywhere from two to ten days to replenish their supply. For this reason, skunks are judicious in their ejection of spray, relying on it as a last resort when warnings fail. Given the chance, skunks are much more likely to take the route of avoidance. Predators disregarding the signals will discover that skunks can be highly accurate in a target range of about 2 m (6 ft), though they have been known to shoot as far as 4.5 m (15 ft). The scent itself can be detected as far away as 1,500 m (1 mile).

Not all spraying episodes are equally potent. Skunks will occasionally engage in a more subtle reminder, releasing just a tiny waft, which some skunk enthusiasts refer to as 'whiffing'.

Chemical research on skunk spray in the past was patchy at best, most likely because few scientists wanted to get up that close, and those who did found their results were far from conclusive. Early research on the chemical composition of skunk spray was performed and reported in 1862 by Dr Swarts in Germany. This was confirmed in 1879 by another German researcher, Dr O. Löw, who was teaching in the u.s. in the 1870s and bravely collected samples of skunk secretion during a trip to Texas, despite objections from his colleagues. Back in New York, his chemical tests came to an abrupt halt when the entire institution demanded that he cease and desist because of the insufferable smell.[13] But a somewhat more intrepid chemist, Thomas B. Aldrich of the Laboratory for Physiological Chemistry at Johns Hopkins University, managed to further his stinky research and published reports of his studies in 1896 and 1897, detailing his findings on the anal gland secretions of *Mephitis mephitica*, which he called 'the common skunk'. In the mistaken belief that toxic properties of some skunk spray compounds could prove fatal, he surmised, 'The substance is a powerful anaesthetic, and has also been used as an antispasmodic. When inhaled without the admixture of a large amount of air the victim loses consciousness, the temperature falls, the pulse slackens, and, if the inhalation were prolonged, the results would doubtless prove fatal.'[14]

The anaesthetic properties purported by Aldrich were relied on heavily in a report from Virginia Agricultural and Mechanical College's Dr Conway in 1881 recounting a prank in which two or three students forced another student to inhale the 'perfume' from a skunk. Though Conway was uncertain exactly how much the student had inhaled, he did detail the young man's condition: 'A total unconsciousness, relaxation of the muscular system, extremities cool, pupils natural, breathing normal, pulse 65, temperature 94'. It took an hour to revive the boy, who complained of a headache that had gone the next morning.[15]

Contemporary research led by chemist William Wood, who was brave enough to take a closer sniff, reveals a more accurate picture of skunk spray chemistry. Wood reports that the seven major volatile components comprising skunk secretion fall into one of two major chemical compounds. The first three are thiols, also known as 'mercaptans', which are classified with organic chemical compounds resembling alcohols and phenols,

YE GODS! IT'S A SKUNK.

Even armed men are no match for the skunk: 'Ye Gods! It's a Skunk', a popular cartoon from the 1880s.

CRISSY, THE SKUNK WOMAN

Chrissy Hand of Howe, Indiana, was known as 'The Skunk Woman', and lived happily with half a dozen skunks who were, in a journalist's words, 'fully-equipped specimens'.

but which contain a sulphur molecule in lieu of oxygen. Wood's forensic foray revealed that two of the thiols, in particular, (E)-2-butene-1-thiol and 3-methyl-1-butanethiol, are the odiferous culprits in skunk spray. Contrary to common lore, these offending thiol molecules are not the same as the molecules constituting other distasteful sulphurous smells (such as human flatulence and bad breath). They also differ from the stinky sulphur compounds blamed on the yeast in wine making. The third thiol in skunk secretion is less volatile and does not activate our olfactory receptors.[16] The thioacetate derivatives of the three thiols are less powerful than the thiols themselves. However, because the derivatives can be readily converted through hydrolysis, or the addition of water, they are responsible for the disappointing fact that dogs who have been bathed following a dousing by skunk spray will often succumb to a stinky relapse in humid or wet weather. Though tomato juice was long considered the go-to remedy for companion animals who had been 'skunked', its effects are, at best, minimal and temporary. When asked about the seventh ingredient in skunk spray, chemist Paul Krebaum responds: 'As to the 2-methylquinoline, I guess you'll have to ask a skunk . . . nobody seems to know why it's there.'[17]

Krebaum is credited with developing the now authoritative and well-publicized home remedy for neutralizing the smell of a skunked dog. The formula is composed of common household items and is worth memorizing:

950 ml (1 quart) of 3 per cent hydrogen peroxide (the 3 per cent is very important, as a larger percentage could be dangerous to pets)
1 cup (180 g) baking soda
1 teaspoon liquid soap

The hydrogen peroxide and baking soda serve as oxidizing agents to transform the stinky thiols into odourless sulphonic acid compounds. The mixture should be applied immediately with a sponge or cloth to sprayed areas, avoiding the animal's eyes and nose, and the animal should be hosed off, with reapplication, if necessary. But the treatment comes with a warning: the concoction should never be mixed in advance, bottled and stored, as the contents can explode. For those willing to shell out a few bucks, ready-made commercial products requiring a little mixing of bottled ingredients are also available. Some dog owners have plugged the success of bathing a skunked dog in popular soft drinks while still others claim that various brands of mouthwash and apple cider vinegar are also curative. But their efficacy is unproven and unlikely, since they lack what Krebaum asserts are the necessary oxidizing agents.[18]

Not all skunk spray is equal. Spotted skunk secretion contains the thiols and thioacetate derivatives of striped skunk spray, but none of the thioacetates. And the secretions of the hog-nosed skunk differ from those of his spotted and striped cousins – the particularly stinky 3-methyl-1-butanethiol is absent. But because hog-nosed skunk spray contains a thioacetate derivative of the major thiol also present in striped skunk spray, Wood postulates that hog-nosed and striped skunks may be more closely related to each other than either is to the spotted skunk. Ironically, the skunk's best defence may also be his greatest liability because negative misconceptions often lead to fatal consequences for the skunk. Despite popular belief, skunks do not spray out of spite; skunk spray does not permanently blind a person; nor does skunk spray contain rabies, despite an old moniker for skunks as 'hydrophobia cats', used in certain North American regions.[19] While rumours periodically circulate that skunk spray killed a dog, there is no confirmed evidence, and some alleged spray

Nature's Miracle Skunk Odor Remover.

deaths have ultimately been attributed to other causes, like old age. But the claims have piqued the curiosity of a group of scientists who have recently launched a study to determine whether skunk spray can ever be fatal.

Despite the skunk's preference for avoiding conflict and preserving the spray for real emergencies, the mere presence of a skunk is apt to provoke consternation and even extreme action. Back in 1931, President Calvin Coolidge did nothing exceptional when he took his double-barrelled shotgun and mephitic matters into his own hands one evening after a neighbour's barking dog called his attention to a lone skunk out wandering across the street from his home in Plymouth, Vermont. Although it seems the skunk was simply minding his own business, 'Mrs Coolidge focused a flashlight on the skunk . . . [while] Mr Coolidge drew a steady bead and pulled the trigger. The skunk dropped.'[20]

The terror of skunk smell was served up for a little comic relief in 1947 in a newspaper article that jocularly reported of a skunk ambling onto a baseball diamond during an Eastern Shore League game in Delaware. As players fled in dread, the umpire was overheard remarking to one of the coaches, 'I've argued with a lot of things, but darned if I'm going to get spat on.' Eventually the skunk moseyed on without incident, and the game resumed.[21]

While most ground animals have learned to give the skunk a wide berth, two aerial predators – the great horned owl and sometimes the red-tailed hawk – appear olfactorily challenged. Though skunks aren't their first choice of food, they will feast quite happily on skunk, not caring one whit that their feathers and even their nests will reek of musk for days after. It is also thought that aerial attacks may catch skunks by surprise, leaving little time to spray. And while most ground predators have learned to leave skunks alone, some, like coyotes or red foxes, when pressed by hunger, have been known to pursue.

Even so, skunks offer their most dangerous predators the same series of cautionary signals before releasing spray: a quick charge, followed by stomping and dragging of the front feet. Some speculate that domestic dogs misinterpret these motions as a playful invitational bow, leading them to ignore the danger. When a skunk raises her tail, it's a clear sign to run, but dogs, unlike other animals that have grown wiser over the generations, haven't learned the lesson and end up the losers in a canine–skunk encounter.

In a recent study, scientists concluded that the skunk's colour patterns might serve as much more than just a fashion statement, and act as an early warning system to predators. Warning coloration, known as aposematism (from the Greek meaning 'to

Striped skunk (*Mephitis mephitis*). It is now thought by some scientists that the skunk's warning stripes function as a sign alerting potential predators to the actual source of danger.

warn away'), exists throughout the animal kingdom, notably among certain flamboyantly coloured insects, reptiles and amphibians. The opposite of camouflage, bright colour makes an animal conspicuous, as seen with venomous snakes or poisonous frogs. Because the skunk's oversized anal glands in action can spray particular targets, the warning stripes and spots, scientists believe, don't just deter potential predators, like the occasional brave rattlesnake or bold bobcat, but may actually direct their eyes to the skunk's anal region.[22]

Skunk Fusion, a product used by bow-hunters as a cover scent, disguises human smell. Commercially made and sold in the u.s., it provides a two-part synthetic camouflage for hunters tracking deer. Advertising copy promises that the 'Intense odor confuses game without alerting'. Photographs depict male hunters squatting next to the carcasses of bobcats, deer and wild boar as testimony to the success of the odiferous cover.

The skunk's exceptional defence may explain why the skunk appears confident and self-assured. A concluding moment in the young adult novel *Skunk Scout* illustrates this. Having left the safe urban world of San Francisco's bustling Chinatown, Teddy joins his uncle on a wilderness camping trip to Mount Tamalpais. He ponders the novelty and perils of wild animal encounters, strange flora and bad weather, mentally contrasting his outdoor adventures with the safer comforts of home. A final confrontation with a skunk in his tent leaves Teddy to observe, 'I should have known Mother Nature would have one last zinger for me . . . The skunk hoisted his tail like a victory flag. Waving it proudly behind him, he marched off into the bushes.'[23]

Armed with a peaceful apparatus for discouraging potential predators, pacifist skunks go about life assuming their defence is pretty much foolproof. This logic fails when it comes to roads and vehicles. Skunks have not yet evolved to fear or flee from cars. Their mistaken assumption is that the motorized predator will respect the warning, which is why they remain indifferent to approaching danger. As habitat disappears, and traffic density increases, roadway skunk fatalities continue to rise.

4 Commodified Skunk

Because they are economically valuable, skunks have been exploited in various ways. At one time, skunk pelts were a highly prized and valuable commodity in the fur market. The perfume industry also profited from musky animals like skunks. In addition to being sold in the thriving global commerce for animal parts used for traditional medicines and aphrodisiacs, the skunk has also been a staple of non-commercial home remedies for a range of illnesses. The genuine affection felt by owners of pet skunks towards their animals might appear to be worlds away from the financial incentives behind commercial profiteering, but this industry also depends on skunk exploitation and the breeding and selling of skunks and other wild animals.

In *Fur, Fortune, and Empire*, environmental historian Eric Jay Dolin argues that the profit potential of wild fur-bearing animals in the Americas was the engine of the New World conquest. More so than the ideology of 'Manifest Destiny', the profitable fur industry drove the westward expansion of the United States.[1] The roots of fur trading extend back to the practices of First Nations people in Canada, who were already trading animal furs among themselves long before European conquest. When French traders arrived, they exchanged guns and trinkets for valuable furs like mink, otter and beaver. Beaver hats for men became extremely fashionable in Europe.

Though somewhat in decline after pressure from animal advocates, the fur industry still thrives, with fur farms and fur coats remaining highly prized and considered elegant by some.

Boy and girl enjoying their pet skunk, *c.* 1920–40, photograph negative, gelatin on nitrocellulose sheet film.

The French defeat by the British led to the loss of New France in 1760, shifting the North American fur trade's main European destination from Paris to London. Though the fur trade had flourished when Native peoples still controlled their own land, over time the business began a slow collapse, in part because of changes in fashion, and in part because success had depended so much on the particular trapping skills of Indians.

It is no coincidence that America's first multi-millionaire made his fortune in the fur trade. In the late sixteenth century German immigrant John Jacob Astor began importing furs from Canada to his fur-goods store in New York for export to Europe, and established the American Fur Company in 1808. Astor even shipped furs to Guangzhou (Canton), China, supplementing his fur fortune by dealing opium and investing in Manhattan real estate. In 1810–12 Astor financed the second overland expedition westward to the Pacific Ocean (the first was the 1804–6 expedition of Lewis and Clark). Astor's fur empire sought control over both the Columbia River (Oregon) and the Great Lakes region. In 1822

Astor's American Fur Company located its new headquarters on Michigan's Mackinac Island, once the sacred place of the Anishinaabe tribes. It is unlikely that the enterprising Astor gave any thought to occupying traditional Anishinaabe sacred lands, or that he would know anything of the stories (*aadizookaanan*) of the great Skunk Spirit, Aniwye, which had been told and retold for generations.

The pelts of beaver, otters, seals and buffalo composed the main sources of profit for the early fur trade; not until the mid-nineteenth century did skunk fur, prized for its beauty, emerge as a highly lucrative commodity, particularly once tanners discovered ways to remove the lingering smell in a complex process that sometimes included degreasing pelts with kerosene and rinsing in saltwater.[2]

In the 1800s skunk fur was 'harvested' by trapping, killing and skinning in the United States, eventually exceeding production of muskrat fur. Even into the mid-twentieth century, skunk fur coats and hats enjoyed popularity, particularly among women. Given the lingering reputation for stench, skunk fur was often disguised and sold under deceptive names like 'marten' or 'American/Alaskan/midnight sable'.[3]

A United States Department of Agriculture bulletin for farmers from 1917, written by a biologist, charted the rising importance of the skunk as a valuable North American natural resource at that time, offering a snapshot of the skunk market about one century ago. The skunk pelt, along with that of muskrat and mink, 'has great intrinsic value and the demand for it has not yet fully developed'. In fact, the skunk 'stands second in importance among the fur animals of the United States, the total value of the annual catch being exceeded only in the case of the muskrat'.[4]

Historically, one of the most popular markets for skunk skins was found in London, since the fur didn't always pass the smell test in the U.S. The scarcity of dark furs like the prized Russian sable meant that skunk pelts, particularly those that were mostly black, played a central role in the European fur market. As processes for ridding pelts of their odour continued to improve, the skunk fur market enjoyed increasing popularity in the early twentieth century. At the time, skunk fur was making U.S. trappers about $3 million every year.

Trapping was considered the most efficacious method for catching skunks, since skunks were easy to lure and shooting them ruined the pelt. Once caught, skunks were typically killed with a sharp blow against the back to paralyse their hindquarters, or strangled with wire nooses. Drowning boxes provided another option. If no water was available, trapped skunks were asphyxiated

A close-up of a section of skunk fur, showing its shiny, coarse texture.

inside the box, a preferred method for killing, because 'the animals die quickly and without struggle'.[5]

The discovery that skunks could be successfully raised in captivity allowed for more control over increased supply, and reduced problems associated with wild trapping. One expert believing the skunk would become an important source of profit predicted that 'Within a few years the prices of this fur will probably be more than doubled', particularly if captive raising were combined with 'intelligent management'.[6]

North Americans were not the only ones jumping on the skunk fur bandwagon. In 1922 the *Illustrated London News* ran a story replete with photographs of 'a new open-air industry' about 'fur-ranching in England'. The skunk farm 'on the borders of

Fur of skinned skunks and other mammals killed in the wild.

Dartmoor' specialized in black skunk fur by eliminating patterns of white through selective breeding.[7] Approximately 100 skunks lived free-range on Dartmoor behind wire fencing, where kennels and dens and feeding areas had been established, and where the keepers could walk among the tame skunks because 'To love the animals and make pets of them is one of the necessities.'[8] But Dartmoor was not the first UK attempt at competing with the American skunk-fur business. A fur farm appeared in 1913 in the Cheviot Hills of Northumberland, where the animals were touted as 'quite as good as any reared or trapped in America'.[9] But the start of the First World War put an end to a promising lucrative business as 'the stock was lost through inexpert attention'.[10] In 1923 a New Zealand newspaper enthusiastically reported the promise of English skunk farming on Dartmoor to supply the home market.[11] And an article in 1924 from anglophone Quebec, under the headline 'Odorless Skunks', provided an update on the progress of the Dartmoor farm, noting that 'fur-farming has spread to the British Isles' on Dartmoor, 'where there are strong breezes' to offset the 'ill-savored smell'.[12] In fact, it wasn't the breezes at all, but the de-scenting surgeries performed on the kits that 'will produce fine furs free from odor'.[13] The following year another Dartmoor story made its way into the *Singapore Free Press and Mercantile Advertiser*, where it was reported that 'the Dartmoor experiment is being carried out on a generous scale, considerable capital being involved.'[14] Both the climate and terrain of Dartmoor were credited with contributing to the quality of fur and the health of the animals. The number of skunks had reportedly grown to 1,000, with a plan to double or triple that figure. It was also noted that in contrast to some other fur-bearing animals, like 'the faithfully-mated silver foxes, the skunks mate more or less promiscuously, and the sexes are allowed to run in merry parties together'.[15] Finally, the article rather delightfully offers the erroneous detail that 'The skunk is an interesting link between the weasel and the badger.'[16]

But regardless of locale, skunk farming was not always successful, and breeding of skunks typically produced mixed results. Some breeders bemoaned spending large sums of money to no avail. Many who made money from skunks ended up selling them for breeding purposes.

Enthusiasm for the potential value of skunks was tempered by another obstacle as well, which had not initially been taken into account: the passing of legislation requiring furriers to specify precisely which kinds of furs consumers were purchasing. Given the negative associations with skunks themselves, it didn't take long for the skunk-fur industry to fall apart.

Additionally, increasing pressure from animal advocates and protection laws, starting in the 1980s, may also be credited with reducing the commercial popularity of animal fur in general. As the cruelties and suffering of animals used in the fur industry were publicized through pictorial campaigns, demand for alternatives grew. Various synthetic materials, sometimes referred to as 'faux fur', provided easy and cheaper substitutes. However, labelling laws are still not fully successful, particularly with regard to imported clothing. Investigations have repeatedly uncovered real animal fur mislabelled as faux, or dog fur being sold as 'raccoon', in consumer clothing, in violation of the u.s Fur Products Labeling Act of 1951 and its 2010 amendment.[17] Fur of a variety of animals, including cats and dogs, has appeared in trim on clothing in major department stores, despite the 'faux' labelling.[18] Even with the gradual decline in the demand for fur, skunk fur continues to be used by a number of contemporary designers like Prada and Fendi, for example, to make coats, capes, handbags and other accessories. Runway models and celebrities still sport coats, accessories and clothing trimmed with skunk fur. Designer

Thomas Ford's 2012 ladies' skunk-fur clutch, which resembles a glossy, long-haired wig, retailed for a whopping $1,660 at Nieman-Marcus. Reality TV star Kim Kardashian has also been photographed in a full-length skunk-fur coat. While it's easy to understand admiration for the elegance of a beautiful skunk-fur coat, a thoughtful person will find it difficult to ignore the fact that 40 to 60 skunks had to suffer and die for its creation.

However, the fashionable skunk also makes appearances without injury to anyone. A harmless trend known as 'skunk hair' evolved, as exemplified by cartoon fur-villainess Cruella De Vil, who gleefully sports the two-toned black-and-white striped hairdo in the Disney animation based on Dodie Smith's novel *The Hundred and One Dalmatians*. An American clothing store calling itself, 'SkunkFunk' sells hip lines of fashionwear, with colour and patterns offering variations on the skunk's black-and-white fur.

Still from the Disney film *101 Dalmatians* (1996). In this live-action remake of the animated film, actress Glenn Close sports 'skunk hair' as a symbol of her evil nature.

In truth, the skunk, when left to his own devices, can be 'a farmer's best friend', with his particular predilection for pesky crop pests like cicadas, locusts, crickets, cutworms, army worms (destructive to grains and grasses), tobacco worms that also attack tomatoes and white grubs with a fondness for strawberries and potatoes. Though some birds will devour white grubs that surface after soil has been cultivated, skunks will actually dig the little critters right out of the ground, locating them with their keen sense of smell.

In the Rocky Mountain locust invasions of the late nineteenth century, skunks were the 'principal mammal that destroyed these insects' so that, in the grateful words of the u.s. Department of Agriculture (USDA) bulletin of 1917, 'the constant service of skunks

Cacomistle and striped skunk group in a 1940s diorama, American Museum of Natural History, New York. Cacomistles are not skunks, but small Central American arboreal omnivores in the Procyonidae family, which includes raccoons.

. . . should not be forgotten.'[19] In fact, the skunk's partiality towards crop-damaging rodents, like mice and rats, makes them even more valuable as a beneficial predator than foxes, badgers, mink and weasels.

Thanks to grateful New York hop growers, who heralded the 'constant service of skunks', protective state legislation emerged in the late nineteenth century to limit killing skunks in New York. Slowly, similar laws spread to other states, and variations on protective schemes across the country included close seasons and shorter hunting periods for skunks. In 1913 the Ohio legislature added specific prohibitions against smoking out or taking skunks from their dens, or otherwise engaging in den destruction.

The perfume industry had long relied on the musk of animals like the skunk for the perfect base for its fragrances, to both enrich and propel the scent. Musk from musk deer and civet cat was also used, but because skunks are sometimes mistakenly referred to as 'civets', it's not always clear which animal is being referenced. Traditionally, musk animals were slaughtered for their scent glands, but protection laws restricting the killing served to encourage entrepreneurs to develop synthetics to replace animal musk and turn to non-lethal alternatives. However, 'non-lethal' is not the same as 'no harm', and extracting musk still means that if animals survive the torture of captive life, they are doomed to endure lifelong, cramped confinement in cages barely larger than their own bodies. They will also suffer intrusive procedures that involve regular scraping of their anal glands. While the motive for exploiting skunks to extract the scent is profit, the fragrance industry's indifference to animal suffering is difficult to distinguish from cruelty.

As long as there is demand, supplying musk from the bodies of animals is likely to continue, even as companies employ a mix of synthetics and real animal musk. Many skunk advocates are

convinced that some pet and fur breeders continue quietly to raise skunks for the perfume industry.

How about a tablespoon of skunk oil to cure your toothache, sore throat or laryngitis? If you are an aboriginal inhabitant of the Boreal Forest in the far Northwest in Canada, skunk oil would likely refer to a concoction of spray diluted with water and spread over the gums.[20] For others relying on folk traditions, skunk oil can also refer to rendered skunk fat, and not the spray itself. This version of skunk oil offers the medicinal properties of warming and moisturizing and has been used as a remedy for rheumatism and sore throats. With a thick consistency, it can be applied to chests to relieve the congestion accompanying the common cold.

A White House visitor dressed in her purchased animal fur accompanied by her pet skunk wearing his own coat, 1922, photograph.

In traditional and home remedies around the world, there is a time-honoured practice of fauna used for medicinal purposes. In the New World, skunk musk was favoured by many Native peoples as a healing liniment, and even sold as a balm to early explorers and fur traders at hefty prices. Also known as 'zootherapy', folk medicine practices remain popular even in contemporary times, in part because of the comfort brought by custom and tradition. But it's also the case that pharmaceuticals are expensive and zootherapy is far more cost-effective.

Additionally, consumers of medicinal fauna believe remedies taken from the natural world are safer. A study conducted in Mapimi, a municipality in the Mexican state of Durango, demonstrated that meat of the hooded skunk still plays a significant role in folk medicine, particularly in treating ailments such as asthma, stomach ache and coughs. Folk remedies may be taken in lieu of prescribed medicines, or along with them, and are often administered by healers known as 'chamanes'. In the respiratory category, oil from the hooded skunk had the highest level of fidelity in treatment.[21]

Likely, most people have never heard of the peace-loving skunk's involuntary contribution to the Second World War effort. During that time trappers began selling skunks not just for their fur, but for their fat, which was used to concoct the glycerin necessary in the ammunition for the Browning .50 calibre machine gun.[22] And skunk oil for riot control? Ireland is considering its potential, after the Israel Defense Force successfully relied on it to control crowds.[23]

While skunk meat was reputedly a common component of diet for Native Americans and trappers, it remains controversial today as a food source, even for those who consume game animals. Stigmas attached to eating skunk flesh may explain why it is not available commercially. Data on skunk-eating is elusive and paints a somewhat inconsistent picture: although some people have occasionally turned to skunk meat, often during lean times, the skunk's place on the dinner plate remains relatively rare. On the other hand, dining on skunk is perhaps not a practice to which even those who engage in it will readily admit. With taste closely connected to smell, the negative association of the meat with the smell seems to have caused potential consumers to turn up their noses. However, a cheeky article from the *New York Times* in 1913 flaunted skunk as a delicacy and claimed in its headline that 'Epicures Proclaim the Skunk a Tasty Dish'. The story features an 'epicure and gourmet' at a Fifth Avenue club who is plugging the delights of skunk meat. According to this food expert,

> if New York cooks only knew how to prepare it, skunk meat would be as popular with men who love gamy foods like possum, roast coon and bear steaks as the pelts are with the womenfolk. It seems as if all womankind was wearing his pelt and nobody eating his carcass. It isn't fair to the skunk.[24]

Forty years later, an article about skunks in the popular *Boys' Life* titled 'Part-time Skunkology' echoed the missed opportunity:

> Incidentally, skunks are edible. The Indians ate skunk and so has many a trapper. I tried it, rolling pieces of cleanly-skinned carcass in flour and browning and steaming them in a skillet. The meat is light in color and well flavored. It is better than raccoon or opossum, but a skunk is bony and not as well padded with meat as a rabbit.[25]

In both cases, skunk meat is treated as a speciality appreciated best by those in the know, and described in the spirit of manly epicurean adventure.

The passing in 1952 of the truth-in-labelling law contributed to a further decrease in skunk-fur sales, which left breeders with a surplus of the animal. As if anticipating the future of the exotic pet industry, it was noted in the USDA bulletin of 1917 that skunks might also make 'interesting' pets. In fact, a grainy title-page photograph depicts a barefoot child cuddling a tame skunk on his lap. As predicted, some desperate fur breeders turned to selling skunks for pets, creating a niche market for skunk fanciers in the ever-burgeoning 'exotic' pet market.

Ownership of pet skunks has become increasingly popular in the U.S., Canada, Italy, Poland, Germany, the Netherlands and the UK. A headline in the *Mail Online* from the UK announced: 'Heaven-scent: Why Skunks are Becoming the Latest Must-have Pet'.[26] While some large fur farms may also sell off excess skunks to pet stores, many pet skunks are bred, raised and sold to individuals by private breeders.

Like most 'exotics', pet skunks aren't for everyone, and skunk owners are likely the first to say this. Unlike dogs or cats, wild animals bred in captivity are not particularly suited to the constraints and expectations of human family life. Baby skunks are often sold as young as four to six weeks by licensed breeders to individuals and to pet stores in states like Indiana, Ohio and Florida, where it is legal to do so. Pet stores must have federal permits to sell the animals, and peak sale time is in June, shortly after the kits have been born. Many pet skunks live as members of the household, alongside other companion animals, though for obvious reasons they would pose a danger to small rodents. According to some, skunks can be 'corner-trained', meaning that owners can place a box of unscented cat litter in the spot where a skunk chooses to relieve himself. But skunks have minds of their own and are likely to do what they want wherever they see fit. Pet owners who understand their active charges appreciate that skunks

ECONOMIC VALUE OF
NORTH AMERICAN SKUNKS

DAVID E. LANTZ
Assistant Biologist

FARMERS' BULLETIN 587
UNITED STATES DEPARTMENT OF AGRICULTURE

Contribution from the Bureau of Biological Survey
E. W. NELSON, Chief

Washington, D. C.　　　　　　Issued June 4, 1914; Revised, July, 1917

Show this bulletin to a neighbor.　Additional copies may be obtained free from the
Division of Publications, United States Department of Agriculture

WASHINGTON : GOVERNMENT PRINTING OFFICE : 1917

The cover of an optimistic USDA pamphlet from 1914 touts the economic value of raising skunks as pets.

are determined and headstrong. Despite 'domestication', pet skunks retain the needs and desires of their wild counterparts, like digging, clawing and biting. Most pet skunks are de-scented as kits, since a fully loaded pet skunk is not for the faint-hearted.

Before being sold as pets, young skunk kits are typically de-scented by the breeder. An innocuous-sounding lay term, the procedure is performed without anaesthesia and can last up to 30 minutes. The mercaptan-producing glands inside the anus are secured with forceps and then sliced off. Despite claims by devotees that this involves minimal pain, de-scenting is condemned as cruel by animal advocates not only for the procedure itself, but because de-scented skunks have also been stripped of their main defence, making an escaped de-scented skunk vulnerable to predators. In the UK, protective legislation forbidding the de-scenting of pet skunks since 2006 initially caused some decrease in the ownership of pet skunks. But Ireland, which has no such prohibition, now offers the supply to meet the demand.

For more mature skunks, there is also the much rarer possibility of a 'bilateral anal gland sacculectomy', which involves surgically removing the skunk's grape-sized anal glands while the animal is under anaesthesia. Most vets are neither trained nor willing to perform this procedure, and the ones who might be inclined to do so will not attempt this after the animal is more than three months old. One U.S. vet who agreed to perform the surgery lamented that his animal hospital was made uninhabitable by the stench for weeks after.

Skunks in captivity require special care, exercise, attention and patience to remain healthy and happy. Maintaining the skunk's good health requires careful attention to reproducing its omnivorous diet and ensuring it gets proper exercise. Skunks are entertaining, but do not make easy pets. Their fondness for digging can prove inadvertently destructive to carpeting, furniture and walls. Though only wild spotted skunks climb trees, pet-skunk owners report skunks being agile enough to find their way onto tables and countertops, where they are apt to get into mischief, such as opening refrigerator or cupboard doors. Equipped with restless curiosity and a powerful sense of smell, skunks are likely to follow their noses into trouble no matter where they live.

For better or for worse, the exotic-pet trade thrives as human beings indulge their longings to live with wild animals. Years ago, if you wanted a pet skunk, you could order one from the Sears & Roebuck catalogue. Now you would be more likely to contact a breeder who specializes in captive-bred wildlife. Advertisements by pet-skunk breeders promising the joys of skunk-keeping proliferate, pet-skunk sales are still high in the U.S., and websites devoted to the care and keeping of pet skunks abound. The ethics of owning wild animals like skunks, even those specifically bred as pets, are complicated. There is very little difference in the personalities and behaviours of wild and pet skunks: a skunk is a skunk is a skunk. And deciding who lives as a companion to humans and who ends up as fur trim on a jacket makes for an interesting meditation.

Many major and minor zoos include skunks in their roster of exhibits. Skunks in captivity can often be seen pacing, a sign of stress. In the wild, skunks easily roam up to 3 km (2 miles) or more a day. More commonly, zoo skunks are used as 'animal ambassadors' in public education programmes that encourage visitors to interact more intimately with the animals they are learning about.

The rationales for keeping unusual pets are probably as numerous and specialized as the individuals involved. For some, it affords an imagined proximity to the wild, and may even introduce a more subtle element of 'danger' within the domestic space. For others, the appeal lies in the novelty and status of owning an 'exotic', or in 'taming the wild'. At a recent gathering of skunk aficionados, I met a devoted skunk owner whose beloved skunk accompanies him everywhere, including to noisy, crowded NASCAR (stock-car racing) events, where she curls up quietly in his arms. Skunk enthusiasts extol the beauty and affectionate natures of their pets. Skunks are funny and charming. Their owners can purchase toys and walking harnesses. Contrary to lore, skunks are exceptionally clean animals. Even so, owners are often urged to bathe their skunks periodically using shampoos designed for the long, shimmering fur. For some, living with a skunk is one of the greatest pleasures of life. Many skunk owners testify that there is nothing sweeter than cuddling in bed with a skunk.

For others, the reality of owning a destructive and mischievous skunk does not align with the fantasy. Under the best of circumstances, keeping skunks, even those bred and raised in captivity, raises both logistical and ethical questions. The nineteenth and early twentieth centuries saw a renewed interest in the natural world, as well as a rise in concern for animal welfare. The literary writing that emerged with animals and nature at its centre often inadvertently fuelled a romanticized or sentimentalized view of the animal–human connection.

One of those whose work stood so accused was Ernest Thompson Seton. In a book that ended up at the centre of the nature-writing controversy, Seton described his years of keeping pet skunks:

> Just now I have about sixty. I keep them close to the house and would let them run loose indoors but for the possibility of some fool dog or cat coming around, and provoking the exemplary little brutes into a perfectly justifiable endeavour to defend themselves as nature taught them. But for this I should have no fear. Not only do I handle them myself, but I have induced many of my wild-eyed visitors to do so as a necessary part of their education. For few indeed there are in the land to-day that realize the gentleness and forbearance of this righteous little brother of ours, who, though armed with a weapon that will put the biggest and boldest to flight or disastrous defeat, yet refrains from using it until in absolute peril of his life, and then only after several warnings.[27]

Quick to denounce Seton's writings as sentimental was the naturalist John Burroughs. The gist of Burroughs's criticism was that, like Jack London with his adventure dog stories, Seton was

Ernest Thompson Seton's daughter shown with pet skunks. Plate XXIV from 'The Well-Meaning Skunk' chapter in Seton's *Wild Animals at Home* (1913).

promoting a skewed and romanticized view of wild animals, a 'sham natural history' and 'yellow journalism of the woods':

> [The] line between fact and fiction is repeatedly crossed and . . . a deliberate attempt is made to induce the reader to cross too . . . Mr Thompson Seton says in capital letters that his stories are true and it is this emphatic assertion that makes the judicious grieve.[28]

But Seton was persistent in his views that wild animals would adapt readily to life with humans. As if anticipating the sceptics, he offered proof of his skunks' amiability in a photo of his daughter playing with their unaltered skunks, accompanied by this observation: 'I present a picture of my little daughter playing among the Skunks, and need add only that they are full-grown specimens in full possession of all their faculties.'[29]

Impressive dentition of a white-backed skunk, as illustrated in the 1850s.

Though skunks arguably may be easier pets than their larger wild brethren, they can still be aggressive, particularly with biting. One skunk owner attests, 'Their teeth are like razors.'[30] Some owners will put their skunks through a rarer procedure called 'de-fanging', an extraction some advocates classify as mutilation. The small mouths of skunks are equipped with 32 teeth, the same number as ours. Their sharp fangs can cause dangerous bites to humans, with a risk of infection. While it is illegal to keep skunks in the majority of states in the u.s., and then usually only with a licence, Britain has no such prohibitions. Licensing laws in the u.s. affect where and how pet skunks can be kept, and anyone raising skunks must hold a usda licence.

Mention skunk diet in a room of skunk owners, and you are likely to hear a variety of opinions on meeting a skunk's health and dietary needs. In addition, many pet skunks end up overweight, creating numerous health issues. Finding a suitable veterinarian for any so-called 'exotic' can be a challenge. Medications and procedures that may be appropriate for animals like dogs and cats could be deadly to a skunk.

A pet hog-nosed skunk freely roams his house.

The exotic pet trade consists of both legal sales and an underground black market. The latter operates outside the law and may involve unlicensed and unregulated breeding operations, the sale of dangerous animals prohibited by law, and the kidnapping of animals, usually babies, from the wild. Therefore it is important to distinguish between keeping wild animals who have been specifically bred and sold legally as pets, and those who are native 'wildlife' and fall under the protection of state and federal laws. In the u.s., animal laws, at both state and federal levels, govern these distinctions very differently, and local laws may be even stricter. A majority of u.s. states have banned keeping any wild animal, including the skunk, even those bred in captivity as pets.

Skunks bred as pets have typically been specifically manipulated to produce colours and patterns that would never exist in the wild. Popular pet-skunk colours are descriptively marketed: chocolate chip or swirl, champagne, cream, apricot, albino, smoke, violet, lavender and blonde.

While skunks bred for pets do not carry rabies, skunks are often aggressive towards strangers. For this reason, many skunk-breeders advise potential owners not to let anyone else handle or touch the skunk. Currently there is no rabies vaccine approved for skunks, in part because of the expense involved in developing one for such limited use.

The human–animal bond does not easily limit itself to the animals conventionally deemed suitable companions, and the chance connection between human and wild animal can and does happen, in real life as well as in fiction. Even so, relationships with humans, even if well-intentioned, can prove as dangerous to the animals as they can to the humans. A news account from 1921 recounts the friendship between a young boy and a wild skunk. In Middleton, New York, the child became attached to a baby skunk he met near his home and made a pet of him, allowing the skunk to follow him throughout the village 'as if he were a dog'. For reasons the article does not make clear, the parents sold the skunk to a dealer of furs, leaving the boy 'almost inconsolable'.[31]

Although most exotic pet-owning endings aren't as tragic as this one, frequently the animal does not conform to fantasies of loyalty and mutual affection, and the consequences for the animal can be grave. Still, those in the exotic-pet trade promote the notion that the breeding and sale of wild animals is naturalized and mutually beneficial. Author and educator Constance Taber Colby writes with great affection about her own vicissitudes of living with the baby skunk she purchased for her family in the 1970s from a Manhattan pet store, describing him as initially being 'about as friendly as a baby wasp'. The acquisition of the skunk followed on the heels, she explains, of a series of sad pet disasters, including a rabbit, mice and a bird. Though she describes the choice of a skunk as 'logical', it is sometimes challenging to understand from her description exactly what logic was applied. The skunk Secret's unhappiness pervades the book, underscored by his aggression and attempts to hide, even as the tales of mischief and misunderstanding are written in a highly cheerful style. Following two failed escape attempts after the family moved from the city, Secret finally succeeds in making his exit. The ending for Secret is speculative, as Colby imagines that Secret might be making a new home in the woods behind their Connecticut farmhouse. But the realities for an escaped pet skunk are likely to be much harsher, as domesticated wild animals are not prepared for the rigours of outdoor living, and a de-scented skunk would have no defence. What is more likely is that Secret died an unpleasant death from either predation or starvation. 'Our lives are undeniably easier now that he is gone', she concedes. While this book was hailed as a heartwarming tale of cross-species love, it also reveals the complexities and heartbreaks involved in owning a wild animal.[32]

Of course, not all pet skunks meet the same fate as Secret, and many pet skunks seem to adapt well to life among humans who have the patience and time to understand and honour their needs. Those who do so claim the rewards are huge.

5 Mythological and Spiritual Skunk

Because the New World skunk would have been unknown in the ancient Middle East and Europe, neither the sacred scriptures of the Abrahamic faiths nor Graeco-Roman myths mention skunks. Leviticus chapter Eleven identifies various creatures, including several members of Carnivora, as 'unclean animals' who may not be eaten. But an amusing typesetting error in the 1950 edition of the Confraternity Old Testament transformed 'skink' (a lizard) into 'skunk' (Leviticus 11:30), placing the skunk among the unclean animals 'that swarm upon the ground', until the text was corrected.[1] Perhaps this brief, but belittling, representation in the Old Testament further amplifies the skunk's precarious status as 'most misunderstood mammal'. The skunk also makes an unexpected appearance in an idiosyncratic rewriting of the Bible intended to reflect contemporary idioms, where Reverend Eugene Peterson took liberties with the cormorant and bittern mentioned in the King James version of Isaiah 34:11, swapping them respectively for vultures and skunks as witnesses to the Lord's destructive wrath.[2]

But the skunk's absence from Old World lore and sacred texts is counterbalanced by a remarkable abundance of New World story and myth featuring the skunk. Non-Native ignorance and misinterpretations of the diversity and nuances within Native peoples' traditions and cosmologies has led to the philosophies

The Squath, from Oliver Goldsmith, *An History of the Earth, and Animated Nature*, vol. III (1774).

and practices of diverse and numerous indigenous nations spread throughout the two American continents being carelessly lumped together. This ignorance reflects a history of domination and imperialism, including systematic efforts to suppress Native religions and impose Christianity. Outsiders seeking insight into private and sacred rituals and beliefs often failed in translating the untranslatable, resulting in inaccuracies. Multiplicity among the many cultural and religious practices is extensive, but certain common threads run through numerous Native belief systems, including deep connections to the natural world, and the conviction that animals, plants and human beings are interdependent and equal participants in a balanced circle of life. Reflecting an equality of status between humans and wild animals, oral storytelling traditions often feature humans and animals able to assume one another's forms. Even when they are antagonists, animals and humans lead deeply interwoven lives.

Vine Deloria Jr (1933–2005), a Standing Rock Sioux author, theologian and activist, offers this caveat for interpreters:

> Animal stories . . . are fraught with the possibility of misunderstanding unless some effort is made to provide a context in which the stories take place . . . Native North Americans saw themselves as participants in a great natural order of life, related in some fundamental manner to every other living species . . . Human beings had a little bit of knowledge and some basic skills, but we could not compare with any other animals as far as speed, strength, cunning, and intelligence. Therefore it was incumbent on us to respect every other form of life, to learn from them as best we could . . .
>
> Over the centuries, certain birds, animals and reptiles and particular human families were, in most respects, one

intimate family and consequently these families depended upon their animal relatives to warn them of impending dangers or crises of a transitional nature.[3]

A convention within the tradition of oral Native storytelling calls for inclusion, when information is available, of both the name and tribal affiliation of the teller. Attributions will follow each story paraphrased here to acknowledge both personal and tribal stamp of the teller. While narrative strategies in myths may at first appear repetitious and disjointed to the untrained listener, increasing familiarity with mythic idioms will lead the reader to what is 'vibrant and logical'.[4]

A painting of a skunk, 1850s, which would have appeared as a wall painting in an Anasazi Kiva. 'Anasazi' was the Navajo term for 'enemy of our ancestors'; the preferred term is 'Ancient Pueblo peoples' referring to the ancestors of Puebloans living in southwest USA.

From the start, skunks joined rabbits, porcupines, coyotes, foxes, beavers, turtles and owls as important actors in Native American myths and legends. Origin myths such as 'how the skunk got its smell' or 'how the skunk got its stripes' employed similar conceits, a few examples of which will follow. Oral story-telling also transfers important cultural history as well as moral guidance. Skunks show up as actors in versatile roles as villains, tricksters, monsters and heroes. In certain Muskogee Creek myths, for example, skunks showcase aspirations of loyalty to family and protection of loved ones. The Winnebagos, however, viewed the skunk more cautiously, believing that external beauty does not obviate internal ugliness. In fact, a common mythological theme is that displays of perceived disrespect or arrogance come with severe consequences.

A Winnebago skunk origin myth (versions appear in other cultures) recounts a time long ago in a village where a human girl is born with the purest white hair. She is considered beautiful and possibly even holy, and her reputation extends far and wide. Men travel long distances to court her. But the girl is narcissistic and instead spends her days gazing into the water at her own reflection. One day, while rubbing petals into her hair and skin, she is startled by the appearance of an ugly, wrinkled man she does not recognize. When the man approaches and attempts to woo her, the young girl ridicules him for his ugliness and spurns his advances. What she cannot know is that he is Turtle, one of the great spirits, who has disguised himself to test her. Angry over such shabby treatment, he discards his wrinkled skin and reveals himself before her in all his godly glory. As punishment for rejecting a great spirit, she will be transformed into a lesser animal, one who will emit a repulsive smell and drive people from her forever. She immediately shrinks in size and her hair turns black, except for the one single white stripe

The magic of skunks is captured in the sketch *Mephitis Dancing* by Alexis Wreden, 2013.

down her backside, making her the first one of the race of skunks (*gûcge*).[5]

A twist on this tale shows up in a legend attributed to the Abenakis. The basic plot points are as follows. A white skunk who failed to demonstrate proper respect to the revered trickster hero and agent of good, Gluskabi, is singled out to be taught a lesson. As punishment, Gluskabi dumps the black ashes of his pipe all over the skunk's white fur, turning him black. In a gesture of concession, Gluskabi adds white stripes, allowing the skunk to retain some dignity.

The disrespectful skunk surfaces again in an old Tejas (Hasinai) legend. Dissatisfied with the qualities the Great Spirit who created him has given him for protection, the skunk launches a lengthy complaint. The black fur for hiding at night is not enough, nor are the sharp teeth and claws. The more the skunk complains and begs for a characteristic that will frighten others away, the angrier the Great Spirit becomes. Finally the Great Spirit settles on a solution, a scent so strong and foul that no one will bother the skunk. But the protection has a downside; it consigns the skunk to a life of solitude.[6]

Some skunk tales, like two recorded from the Algonquins, provide amusing lessons on clever one-upmanship, like this one featuring a tricky skunk who gets the better of a vain possum. Overly conceited about his beautiful silver tail, the boastful possum insults the skunk: 'O you Skunk over there, you smell so

Large-tailed skunk (*Mephitis macroura*) from J. W. Audubon, *The Quadrupeds of North America* (1851–4).

A medicine bag made from skunk fur and leather.

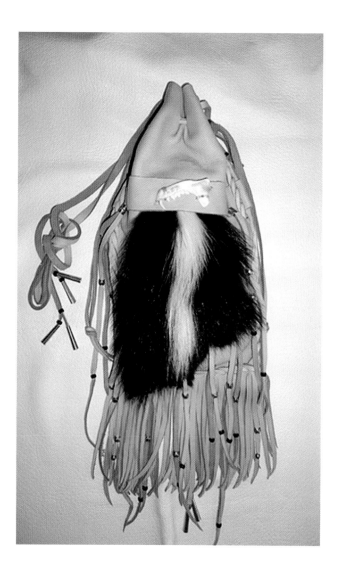

strong that it hurts!' The skunk fires back that the possum had better beware because a dangerous snake is following him. Startled, the possum mistakes his own tail for the snake and takes off running, convinced each time he turns around that the snake is in hot pursuit. He runs so fast and long that eventually his once beautiful tail goes threadbare like a snake's, which explains the hairless tail the possum sports today.[7]

An encounter between Skunk and Grizzly Bear starts out as a friendly rivalry over who is endowed with the most supernatural power. Eyeing Grizzly's dangerous claws, Skunk informs Grizzly: 'my buttocks are also en[d]ued with supernatural power'. Amazed, Grizzly suggests a contest to determine who is telling the truth. Skunk sets off a couple of blasts that kill Grizzly, whom he then magically restores to life. He is quick to point out that he held much of his spray in reserve, and proceeds to demonstrate to Grizzly that he can make a whole lake vanish by aiming his spray at it. In the end, Grizzly is a true believer: 'Now whatsoever you say to me, whatsoever the errand you command me, the same will I do.'[8]

The skunk's special powers also make him, at times, mortally dangerous, as portrayed in the numerous versions of Giant Skunk myths. This particular variation is paraphrased from a telling by Gwen Bear (Maliseet).

Giant Skunk is an enormous monster capable of shooting his spray across oceans. Two brothers, Koluskap and Mikumwesu, paddling downstream in their canoe, have a premonition that they will be confronted by Giant Skunk and his deadly spray. They pull ashore to hatch a plan. While Mikumwesu uses pipe smoke to create a fog and temporarily blind Giant Skunk before he can spray, Koluskap jabs him with a sharpened stick just enough to reduce his size and ensure the skunk will be left with only enough spray to protect himself.[9]

Hog-nosed skunk (*Conepatus mesoleucus*), from Nelson, *Wild Animals of North America*. Despite images of real skunks to the contrary, the mythologized skunk was often assigned not just monstrous proportions, but power beyond imagining, capable of wiping out scores of people with a single blast.

Another Giant Skunk story, from the Ojibwe, involves an even more monstrous human-eating skunk called Aniwye, who kills his human prey by passing gas. When defeated by the hero, Great Fisher (Nanabozho, a North American mustelid resembling a weasel), Giant Skunk is reduced to the small size we know today. Variations on a Cree legend detail the defeat of Giant Skunk by a wolverine, and illustrate the often digressive and non-linear strategies of the mythopoet. This one of particular interest, paraphrased after a telling by Sandy Masty from Whapmagoostui, features an eldest son, Kuikuhâchâu, who lives happily off the land with his family. His companions are game animals and Kuikuhâchâu can assume the form of Wolverine when necessary. Life is good and peaceful. But trouble is brewing in the form of Giant Skunk Wâniyûyâu, who is notorious for murdering whole camps of people.

While out hunting one day, Kuikuhâchâu's younger brother Shikushâpâu, also known as Ermine Man, finds himself confronted by the terrifying Giant Skunk Wâniyûyâu. Though Shikushâpâu escapes by burrowing into the snow, as ermines can do, Wâniyûyâu still knows that Shikushâpâu has been on his trail and seeks revenge. Shikushâpâu returns home and reports the close call to Kuikuhâchâu, who takes immediate action. To protect his family, Kuikuhâchâu relocates them all from their camp to different sites of safety. He always leaves behind a structure called a Shaking Tent where he performs the necessary ceremony to keep track of Giant Skunk's whereabouts. Since Wâniyûyâu can also take on human form, he is able to travel inconspicuously in the winter on snowshoes, killing for pleasure everyone he finds with spray from his deadly scent glands. He is determined to find and kill Shikushâpâu, but arriving at the camp he finds only the Shaking Tent.

Shape-shifting into his skunk form, he raises his tail and shoots a stream of deadly spray at the tent to prove his powers. In the meantime, Kuikuhâchâu keeps his family on the move, warning his two older and slower-travelling sisters Mâtishkûtish (Frog) and Ayik (Toad) to play dead should they catch sight of Wâniyûyâu. While crossing a frozen lake, Frog keeps looking back for Giant Skunk, but Toad doesn't. When Giant Skunk comes upon Toad, she doesn't recognize him and allows him to fall into step with her. She explains that she is fleeing Giant Skunk. Angered by her arrogance in imagining that she could ever escape him, Giant Skunk blinds her with his spray and then kills her. Pleased with himself, he sets off in search of more people to kill. Frog spots Giant Skunk following her and, as planned, changes into a small frog and drops to the ground. Disgusted, Wâniyûyâu decides not to waste his spray on her and leaves her for dead. He embarks on a murderous rampage and Kuikuhâchâu springs into further action by laying a series of traps.

When Wâniyûyâu shows up at their camp, Kuikuhâchâu employs wit and skill to disempower him. Transforming into a wolverine shape, Kuikuhâchâu leaps onto Wâniyûyâu and clamps his jaws over the skunk's anus to seal off the deadly defence. Wâniyûyâu cries out that Kuikuhâchâu is breaking his arrows. Maintaining his grip, Kuikuhâchâu calls for help from his siblings, who stab Giant Skunk into tiny pieces that they then throw into the sea. He instructs his brothers to order the pieces of Giant Skunk to remain that size forever. Now that Kuikuhâchâu has vanquished the violent and sadistic killer, he sets out to assure the fearful community that they are once again safe.[10]

Disrespect and insubordination are punished in another 'pretty, but rude maiden' theme, in this Lenapé tale involving three male characters, Kukhus (Owl), Tamakwa (Beaver) and Shikak (Skunk). Kukhus makes the first attempt to woo a beautiful young woman who has rebuffed all her human suitors. She calls him ugly and refuses to take him as a husband. Likewise with Shikak, only she adds insult to injury by telling him he stinks. Tamakwa tries a different tack. His plan is to gnaw part of the way through a log that serves as a bridge over the creek, in hopes that the next time the beautiful woman comes to retrieve water she will fall into the creek and cry for his help. The woman arrives, falls into the creek as expected and calls out that if Tamakwa were there, he could save her. But when he arrives and asks to be her husband, she insults him, just as she did the others, by calling him ugly because of his big teeth and paddle tail. Tamakwa is crushed and returns to Kukhus and Shikak to tell of his defeat. In the meantime, the beautiful woman drowns because she has refused his help.[11]

In a legend attributed to Mayan origins, a skunk mother and young son have been baptized by Mr Jaguar, creating an important relationship. Mr Jaguar offers to take the little skunk under his wing and teach him to hunt. Fearful that something bad might befall her young son, Mrs Skunk is reluctant. But Mr Jaguar is convincing, and the little skunk begs to go, so Mrs Skunk agrees. The hunting trip takes them a good distance away. After they arrive at the river, Mr Jaguar says he's going to sharpen his 'knife', meaning his claws, and instructs the little skunk to keep an eye out for a deer with antlers. Then he falls asleep. When the little skunk spots the antlered deer, he alerts Mr Jaguar, who makes the kill. They return home with meat for the little skunk's mother. Sometime later, the little skunk and his mother run out of meat. Confidence bolstered by this experience, the little skunk believes he can hunt on his own. Mrs Skunk is worried and cautions him not to go out alone, but the little skunk believes he can succeed if he just does exactly what he saw Mr Jaguar do.

Original watercolour drawing of the of 'American Skunk' (*Mephitis mephitica*), now Striped Skunk (*Mephitis mephitis*), *c.* 1860, for *Zoological Sketches by Joseph Wolf* (London, 1861).

Drawing by Cheyenne artist Tichkematse of a Native American scout, 'Necklace', poking at a skunk with a gun, 1887.

Returning to the river, he sharpens his own 'knife' and waits for the deer. When the deer arrives, he attacks him. But what the little skunk has failed to realize is that he is much too small, and instead of killing the deer, he ends up falling onto his back and dying. His frantic mother sets out to search for him. When she finds him, she mistakenly thinks he's alive and laughing because his mouth is open and his teeth are showing. But when she realizes the truth, her grief concludes the story.[12]

Coyotes, foxes, ravens and monkeys often appear in world legends as trickster figures, but the skunk has also taken up the role. Tricksters may be divine spirits or anthropomorphic animals who live by their own rules and often flaunt conventions. They can also move fluidly across boundaries of gender and animality, and 'afford the narrator an opportunity to flirt with immoral or antisocial temptations'.[13]

The trickster skunk appears in a number of Native myths. For the Klamaths, the skunk is both 'a bad fellow, but an amusing one', and most often characterized 'by his odor, equated with flatus, and his inordinate vanity'. But the skunk can also be violent

106

towards those who do not show him sufficient deference. In one story, five skunks set out to murder anyone who doesn't admire them. Eagle kills four of them, but the surviving skunk shows up at an Eagle clan seance impersonating a shaman, and kills everyone present with his flatus. After abducting Eagle's sister, he is clubbed to death by Eagle. But the skunk is able to revive himself when Morning Star calls.[14]

That more amusing side of trickster Skunk's powers is illustrated in this tale about the hungry Coyote who happens upon Skunk. Coyote has developed a nasty plan to trick the nearby Prairie Dogs and enlists Skunk's aid. Skunk is assigned to play dead, while Coyote lures the unsuspecting Prairie Dogs from their burrows by promising a dance to celebrate the death of their enemy Skunk. The Prairie Dogs are ordered to close their eyes to avoid being transformed into something bad. When the excited Prairie Dogs begin to dance, Coyote starts killing the unsuspecting guests, one by one. As it dawns on one of the Prairie Dogs that they have been duped, he alerts the others, and the remaining survivors disappear to the safety of their burrows. In the meantime, Skunk jumps up, and together he and Coyote gather firewood to cook the dead Prairie Dogs. Because Coyote has no intention of sharing the meat, he concocts a plan to deceive Skunk. Feigning boredom, he suggests that while the meat cooks, they pass the time in a foot race. To even the stakes, Coyote agrees to tie a rock to his foot so he won't automatically outrun Skunk. As Skunk eagerly takes off and gains the lead, Coyote hobbles along, pretending to be left behind. What he doesn't know is that clever Skunk has anticipated his plan, and swiftly ducked into the brush along the way. From there, Skunk watches Coyote stumble by with the rock on his foot. Skunk immediately returns to the fire and carries off the cooked meat to enjoy for himself. After a while, Coyote wonders how Skunk has managed to get so far ahead, and backtracks to the fire. Upon discovering that the meat is missing, he realizes that he's been hoodwinked and flies into a rage. Skunk, watching from his hideout, begins to taunt Coyote by throwing down pieces of Prairie Dog bones. When Coyote objects to Skunk's trickery, clever Skunk insists that he has won the race and therefore the meat rightfully belongs to him.[15]

A Crow Nation variation reverses the initial roles of Skunk and Coyote, with Rabbits joining the ill-fated Prairie Dogs. Coyote plays dead, while Skunk lures out the prey. In this version, Coyote agrees to let Skunk place him on driftwood and fill his ears, eyes, armpits and mouth with slimegrass to mimic maggots. The Rabbits and Prairie Dogs gather around for a closer look at the presumably dead Coyote. Skunk plays along with the ruse and hits Coyote with a stick to dispel any doubts that he is dead. As the Rabbits and Prairie Dogs begin to celebrate their enemy's death, Skunk catches them off guard and sprays them in their eyes, blinding them. This allows Coyote to leap up and beat them to death with the same sticks. As in the previous version, Coyote suggests the foot race while the meat cooks, and Skunk outwits Coyote, this time by hiding in a badger hole while Coyote hurries past. The Crow version of the story ends with Coyote and Skunk becoming mortal enemies, which explains why you will never see a skunk and coyote together.[16]

In Lakota mythology, the tribe believed skunks were powerful because they stood up to danger. Sometimes Lakota warriors heading into battle and wishing to demonstrate their strength to opponents would don skunk-fur ankle bracelets as symbols of their prowess.[17] Some Cherokees believed that the powerful odour of dead skunks warded off disease, and they would hang skunk corpses over doorways for protection.[18]

However, for the Lummi tribe in northwestern Washington, the skunk signified pure evil. According to a legend recounted

by medicine man Isadore Tom, Skunk is sent by a jealous shaman to a nearby village, where he steals food without interference because the inhabitants fear his mortal spray. The 'poisonous gas' comes from a natural mineral spring, the location of which no one but Skunk knows. When the villagers band together and roll a fire-heated rock down the hill over the aggressive Skunk, they fail to kill him. But they do burn his back sufficiently to eliminate his poison, thereby breaking his medicine. This explains the white stripe down his back that distinguishes him from such animals as Fisher and Wolverine who are, by contrast, considered omens of good luck and wealth.[19]

Despite variations on the famous Skunk and Fisher myth (sometimes involving different animal characters), a number of factors remain similar, but the version attributed to the Coeur d'Alene is perhaps one of the most dramatic, adding elements

Texan skunk enjoying his own meaty meal, from J. W. Audubon, *The Quadrupeds of North America*, vol. II (1851).

not present in other versions, including Skunk's role first as a kidnapper and then as a chief (one may recall that Skunk was also a kidnapper in the Klamath story). Skunk and Fisher share a home. Fisher hunts, keeping the best meat for himself, while Skunk receives the lesser parts of the game. Skunk is notorious for disagreeable habits, like the sounds he makes, as well as his smell and his duplicity. A chief sends his daughters, Chipmunk and Squirrel, out in search of meat at the home that Fisher and Skunk share. The girls are warned by their mother that Skunk's meat is never as good as Fisher's. Skunk hides the girls as Fisher returns from a hunt, and then heads outside to eat grass. When Fisher discovers the girls, he decides to take the meat and the girls, and burn the house. When Skunk sees the plume of smoke he assumes it's the Cayuse burning the Coeur d'Alene village. Feigning concern for the welfare of the chief's daughters, he takes off in hot pursuit. When he comes upon them, he resorts to various deceptions and tricks Fisher into the water before squirting his fluid into Fisher's eye. He then steals the girls and makes them his servants. When they escape, he follows them to a village where he kidnaps a baby and squirts his fluid around to gain control. Everyone dies, except for one woman he has only blinded with his spray. In return for restoring her sight with another blast of spray, the power-mad Skunk convinces her to announce his arrival at another village as the new chief. She follows his instructions, pointing out his yellow moccasins, and the stripes on his eyes and the back of his head. He is greeted like royalty, and the village people 'made the noise of transformation and became stars'.[20]

As these stories illustrate, boundaries between humans and animals are often permeable. Traditional Native reverence towards and connections with the natural world led some tribes to claim skunks as 'clan animals'. A clan animal refers to a specific animal from which the particular clan 'has come'. Some clan members may exhibit attributes of the animal, such as the strength of a bear or the wisdom of a crow. A clan animal is often considered to be an ancestor or relative, as revealed in stories passed down that celebrate the ways in which the animal has helped a human being.[21] Tribes with skunk clans include the Creek (the skunk clan is called Kunipalgi or Konepvlke), the Choctaw and the Chickasaw. The Hidatsa also had a Skunk or Polecat Society, which was a ceremonial organization of young women associated with celebrating war honours.[22]

The skunk's reputation is not limited to its own turf, but evokes honourable mention all over the world, as seen in this Bulgarian stamp.

The dream landscape also features skunks. Dream skunks are subject to varying interpretations, sometimes signalling strength and power, or a desire that justice prevail; at other times, the presence of a dream skunk, particularly if he sprays, serves as a warning to repel the undesirable in the dreamer's life, perhaps eliminating something 'that stinks'. The skunk can also signal repressed anger or a situation that needs fixing.

According to Richard Webster, 'the connection between animals and humans is a basic belief of shamanism. The shaman uses his power animal, or guardian spirit, to connect with the animal world to do his work. This frequently happens in dreams.'[23] In some belief systems, like those of the Cocopa of the Colorado River Valley and the Jivaro people of South America, animals can also appear as human beings in dreams.[24]

Skunk symbology includes the skunk as totem. Defining 'totem' can be tricky, but generally totems are natural beings, like plants and animals, associated with the practices of people who traditionally hold that particular natural objects embody special symbolic import for their community. Totems may also refer to animals that are regarded as beautiful or feared or most commonly seen. The word derives from an Algonquin word, *ototeman*, and connotes 'brother-sister kin' relationships outside of political, economic and religious beliefs.[25] Those belonging to

Unlike the aggressive skunk of legend, this curious domesticated hog-nosed skunk calmly investigates his surroundings.

This close-up of a domesticated striped skunk illustrates the beauty and 'life force' each skunk generates.

the same totem retain strong kinship obligations. In some instances, a totem can refer to an imaginary being who functions as a protector or patron saint of a clan or tribe. For North American kin groups, there are usually strong taboos against killing clan animals.[26]

As totem animals, skunks may signify differently, depending on the tradition. The skunk may teach that one does not need to be physically strong or dominant in order to be powerful, and that power can occur in calm moments of self-reliance. Totem skunks often connote peace and solitude and can be associated

with traits of control and self-confidence. Additionally, spiritual value in the gentle demeanour and 'don't bother me' philosophy link the values of respect, dignity, good judgement and self-protection to the skunk. Some shamanistic practitioners believe the skunk offers an excellent example of how to get along in the world and interact with others. The skunk's preference for solitude serves as a reminder that there are times to be with others and times to be alone. But the presence of a skunk may also be a summons to those who are isolated to engage in more positive social interactions. The skunk's harmless but effective defence can be viewed as a metaphor for pacifism, a sign of its aversion to conflict, in concert with the oft-cited Wiccan Rede to 'cause no harm', though it's wise to exercise caution before crossing a person with a powerful skunk totem.

Many traditional Native American beliefs about animals in general, and skunks in particular, have also been incorporated into the practices and philosophies of Western pagan, shamanistic and alternative healing communities, who borrow rituals and language from various cultures. According to Ted Andrews, the skunk's stripe indicates the active flow of the kundalini or life force. (The kundalini has ties to the sexual energies and to the life force active in every aspect of our life processes.) In individuals with a skunk totem, the kundalini is usually already active.[27]

Many Native peoples and traditional cultures ascribe medicinal powers to skunks. The skunk's particular capacity for restoring the human psyche is celebrated by skunk devotee Diane Blount-Adams in *Skunk Medicine*. Drawing loosely on Native American folklore and traditions, she praises the emotional and spiritual benefits of living with the skunks Sequoia and Jeronimo. In her 33 tales, Blount-Adams describes the healing relationship with the two skunks, who teach her the grace of patience, kindness and love. They also serve as spirit guides for recognizing and embracing, she writes, what the Creator has to offer. Blending spiritual journey and humorous anecdote about daily life shared with mischievous and personable skunks, she borrows from Hopi Nation myths and prophecies for the Four Worlds of Creation. According to Blount-Adams, the Second World, Topka, designates, in this order, the skunk, the eagle and the spruce as chiefs over the people.

> The skunk of Hopi legend is a powerful medicine of the supernatural . . . the shaman of the four-legged. Skunk, kolichiyaw, shows the way for all people to walk in peace . . . Skunk brings power to the path walked, strength to detach, awaken and revive for the journey to the mountaintops.'[28]

Blount-Adams's skunks bring solace during a series of health crises. Diagnosed with cancer, Blount-Adams credits playing with Sequoia for her miraculous improvement. While Sequoia is a wild skunk, Jeronimo is a 'fur farm reject' whose fate improves after arriving at Blount-Adams's home, paralleling her own curative journey through mutual healing. The two skunks are 'medicine' for the body and teachers of psychic and spiritual well-being.

According to self-styled shaman Steven Farmer, the appearance of a skunk in your life can signal many things: sticking up for yourself, direct and honest communication, or that 'your sexuality and sensuality are in a heightened state right now, so explore the use of natural scents and essential oils'. Call on Skunk if you're in need of a self-esteem boost, or you need to defend yourself without aggression.[29] Skunks are often viewed positively as power animals able to draw people to each other and even improve sexual response.[30]

While a totem animal is often shared by a community or clan, it can also be personal to one individual. A carving or picture, for example, may serve as a physical representation of a favourite spirit animal. The representation of a totem animal refers not only to the physical being, but to the spirit of the animal. The New Age mainstreaming of some of these traditions has been criticized as appropriation, and viewed somewhat sceptically. But the principle that everyone is born with an animal spirit guide has roots embedded in traditional beliefs and encourages a closer attention to our relationships with animals. When such animals show up, human beings must be receptive to the opportunity and accept their presence, or the animals will simply leave.

6 Never Cry Skunk

Perhaps the only word likely to clear a crowded theatre faster than the shouted warning of 'Fire!' is 'Skunk!' Equally alarming might be a neighbour's announcement that a skunk is ambling into your garden, inspiring terror in even the most intrepid home owner.

Their powerful defence mechanism has earned the skunk the inventive epithet 'chemical warfare on legs'.[1] And four centuries ago, facing the skunk's infernal spray, French missionary Gabriel Sagard christened New World skunks 'les enfants du diable' (children of the Devil).[2] The English word 'skunk' traces its origins by way of *seganku*, the Abenaki word for skunk, to a proto-Algonquian root relating to 'urination', undoubtedly a reference to the skunk's spraying prowess. The Abenaki language was historically spoken by two related nations, the Abenaki and the Penebscot. Abenaki is a polysynthetic language, meaning one that uses 'sentence words'; thus the word *seganku* roughly translates into English as 'he who squirts or urinates'. Some translations and etymologies render *seganku* as the 'urinating fox' or 'squirting fox'. Interestingly, *seganku* can refer to either the small, bushy-tailed animal itself, or the glossy black-and-white fur.[3] Poetic names for the skunk mentioned in H. E. Anthony's *Mammals of America* (1917) include 'wood pussy', an allusion to the skunk's feline appearance, and 'essence peddler'.[4] A skunk by any other name might be colloquially called 'polecat' in the American South, and smell no sweeter.

According to some etymologists, the 'pol' in polecat is a linguistic legacy of the Norman Conquest, deriving from Old French *poulet*, meaning 'chicken', perhaps because polecats will readily kill and eat chickens, as well as chicken eggs.[5] But the first half of 'polecat' might also derive from an Old English word meaning 'foul'.

The 'polecat' appears in both Chaucer and Shakespeare. A young thief with murder on his mind in Chaucer's 'The Pardoner's Tale' justifies his need for poison by claiming it's needed to kill rats that are going after his roosters: 'And eek ther was a polcat in his hawe / That, as he seyde, his capouns hadde yslawe . . .'.[6] Polecats were so despised in Britain for their predation on poultry that they were systematically hunted and killed, almost to the point of extinction at the beginning of the twenty-first century. Conservation efforts in Wales have reversed the trend, and the polecat is slowly making a comeback. Polecat references appear twice in Shakespeare's *The Merry Wives of Windsor*, notably in Ford's volley of recriminations directed at the overweight Falstaff, disguised in women's clothing as Fontana: 'Out of my door, you witch, you hag, you baggage, you polecat, you runyon!' (IV.2) Master Ford's language is strong for the time, and 'polecat' in this context means 'prostitute'. The polecats Chaucer and Shakespeare knew are not the New World skunk (*Mephitis mephitis*), but rather the solid-body mustelid *Mustela putorius*, which makes its home in Eurasia and North Africa. And though firmly settled into the mustelid family, from which *Mephitis* has now been separated, the European polecat shares with his American skunk cousin the familiar reputation as both stinky and sexually promiscuous.

Idiomatic usages of the word 'skunk', particularly in American English, present a chance to further ponder associations between humans and animals. While many comparisons with animals can be complimentary ('clever as a fox'), the use of 'skunk' is generally unflattering. The semantic flexibility of the word 'skunk' makes it polysemous – that is, capable of signifying multiple and even contradictory meanings depending on context. For example, a person who cheats or doesn't pay a bill is a 'skunk', while the triumph of badly beating an opponent in a game is known as 'skunking'.

'Skunk' hurled as an invective towards one's opponents takes on potent proportions, even periodically causing stirs in the political arena. In 1980, during the Abscam scandal (in which FBI agents disguised as Arab oil sheikhs conducted a bribery sting to trap members of the U.S. Congress), U.S. segregationist Dixiecrat Senator Strom Thurmond famously denounced his colleague, U.S. Representative John Jenrette, as a 'lying skunk' after Jenrette informed an undercover FBI agent that Thurmond was willing to take a bribe.[7]

Sometimes 'skunk' is the animal whose name must not be spoken. En route to the hemispheric summit in Costa Rica in 1989, Nicaraguan President Daniel Ortega denounced stepped-up U.S. military interference and covert paramilitary attacks against his country and warned that Nicaragua might have no choice but to take self-defensive measures. In response, President George H. W. Bush modified a common expression by likening Ortega to 'that unwanted animal at the garden party'. Prudent diplomatic advisers felt that invoking 'skunk at the picnic' would be just too over the top.[8] Attacking Nicaragua militarily gave no pause, but uttering the S-word was off limits. The unspeakable 'skunk' seemed beyond the pale of diplomacy, even for countries lacking diplomatic relations, despite the fact that a few years earlier former president Ronald Reagan had not balked at trash-talking the Nicaraguan leader by including him in a round-up of 'the strangest collection of misfits, Looney Tunes and squalid

criminals since the advent of the Third Reich'.[9] And speaking of the Third Reich, various figurines and posters produced during the Second World War depicted Adolf Hitler as a mustachioed skunk.

The phrase 'skunk at the picnic' may refer to someone bold enough either to speak truth to power, or to serve as the bearer of bad tidings. The same idiom served as the title of a thinly veiled 2013 political CIA thriller by L. Britt Snider. But the political skunk has a longer history. Decades before President Bush referred to President Ortega in covertly odious terms, American newspapers in 1927 carried a brief note bearing a London dateline reporting that the Speaker of the House of Commons had ruled that 'it was unparliamentary and ungentlemanly for one man to call another a skunk.'[10] And when U.S. President Abraham Lincoln made the statement 'What kills a skunk is the publicity it gives itself', he was directing his vitriol not towards a single individual, but against the entire institution of American slavery, which he had come to abhor.[11]

Ardent abolitionist and colourful U.S. Representative Thaddeus Stevens of Pennsylvania was known for his sharp wit. Despised by pro-slavery forces for his anti-slavery stance, and for his strong advocacy of African Americans to have an equal stake in the future of the South, Stevens often found himself embattled. When an opponent passed close by him one day and sneered, 'I never get out of the way for a skunk', Stevens stepped to the side and replied, 'I always do.'[12]

The use of 'skunk' to insult someone whose professional behaviour 'stinks' gave rise to a libel case from Wisconsin in 1887. Here are the offending words the defendant had angrily directed against the plaintiff, a local businessman:

I denounce you as only fit to be classed with that repulsive order of creation, the *Mephitis Americana.* If your ignorance

A Second World War propaganda poster, depicting Hitler as a skunk.

121

is as limited as your sense of manhood, honor, and decency appears to be, you will be unable to comprehend the appellation applied to you, and to save you the further humiliation of seeking light from your neighbors, I will translate for your benefit: SKUNK, – a thing as repulsive to the finer sensibilities of man as your low insinuations and business practices are to your fellow-townsmen.

The inherently pernicious nature of the slur linking man to skunk proved incontestable; the Supreme Court of Wisconsin ruled that because the defendant's skunk language was libellous per se, the trial judge had properly instructed the jury that the 'skunk' accusation was defamatory as a matter of law.[13]

'Skunk' holds a no less provocative place in the realm of flora. A popular use of 'Skunk' (with a capital 'S') is slang for a strong (stinky or aromatic, depending on one's perspective and taste) variety of popular but expensive marijuana, particularly the sativa-dominant cannabis strain, which boasts a 10 to 15 per cent level, or higher, of the psychoactive component THC (Tetrahydrocannabinol). The difference between *Cannabis sativa* and *Cannabis indica* is that the former offers an uplifting, more energetic high, whereas the latter induces relaxation and perhaps even couch potato syndrome. Popular among medical marijuana smokers, skunk weed is touted for its purported medicinal abilities to cure everything from poor appetite to headaches. Skunk weed won the *High Times* Harvest Festival award in 1990.[14]

Like other farmers who share and hybridize seeds to improve the quality of a product, early marijuana growers began developing special seeds, some of which were reputedly mixed with strains from places like Nepal and Afghanistan, and from the Netherlands. One of the most notorious growers is an American member of Sacred Seeds, known as Sam the Skunkman (also

ALL SET

known as David Watson). He is reputedly the original distributor of various hybrids and became the CEO, along with a fellow California expatriate, of the company Hortafarm in Amsterdam. Lore surrounding Sam the Skunkman varies, including connections with the Drug Enforcement Agency (DEA) and possible collusion with law enforcement after he was busted in Santa Cruz, California, but he claims to maintain the largest marijuana seed library in the world and is credited with bringing Skunk #1 and other strains like Original Haze into the Netherlands, where it was then cultivated and sold to growers around the world. In 2011 a concerned Dutch Government began the process of reclassifying 'Skunk' as a hard drug because it exceeds the 15 per cent THC limit.[15]

A review in the online journal *Medical Jane* from 2012 touts the benefits of the hybrid strain of marijuana known as Super

Postcard featuring a skunk with Hitler's face, an oft-repeated Second World War meme.

Skunk, which packs a powerful psychotropic punch at 19 per cent THC. The reviewer describes Super Skunk, sold in legalized California medical marijuana dispensaries, as smelling like a blend of Cheddar cheese and sweet skunk smell, and offering up 'an aroma similar to a skunk on steroids'. Though users are advised caution for morning use because of the 'stoney, but uplifting effects', the review concludes that this is one 'awesome strain'.

Used as an adjective for another pleasure-enhancer, 'skunked' or 'skunky' beer describes the breakdown of certain hop oils in beer processing into a chemical that in both composition and aroma resembles skunk smell.

The aptly named skunk cabbage, *Symplocarpus foetidus*, is a Native root medicine associated with bears, which eat the roots. The second half of its name, *foetidus*, describes the strong skunk-like odour. Sometimes known as swamp lantern because of the beautiful golden flowers growing on a spadix (a spike of small flowers) inside the sheath-like spathe, skunk cabbage has a long history of curative uses. Following Native traditions, skunk cabbage has been promoted as a kind of cure-all for everything from epilepsy to coughs. Its healing powers are still touted by contemporary herbalists and alternative medicine practitioners. It is commonly used as an expectorant, narcotic and anti-spasmodic, though parts of the plant are considered toxic to humans because of high levels of calcium oxalate crystals.[16] Skunk cabbage leaves can be crushed and applied as a poultice. The spicy root can also be boiled for tea, known for its ability to calm nerves and cure worms. As an ointment, it reduces skin tumours. The musky skunk-like odour also attracts the insects that pollinate the plants. The Haudenosaunee, a confederation of various Native peoples also known as Iroquois, are said to have used their vast knowledge of healing plants to find many uses for skunk cabbage,

Super Skunk
marijuana plant.

including aiding in women's reproductive health. The broad oval and heart-shaped green leaves are sometimes called Indian waxed paper, because they have traditionally been used to dry berries or prepare food.

A 'skunk word', in urban slang, signifies the negative speech of either a bigot or the highly sanctimonious. The 'skunk eye', an old term describing a particular raised-eyebrow look of disdain, was popularized by late-night American talk show host David Letterman. According to a dictionary on British slang, 'skunk' is a mildly derogatory term for a person from Newcastle upon Tyne, and more particularly a fan of Newcastle Football Club, whose team colours are black-and-white stripes.[17]

Variations on skunk slang phrases run from the mildly offensive to the deeply scatological, usually involving sexual acts or body parts. Within urban slang, 'skunk' can sometimes serve as a term of endearment for a woman. Yet in another context it may refer to a girl considered to be 'slutty', again linking skunks to sexual promiscuity. Sexual connotations of 'skunk' seem endless, as 'skunk sex' may refer generally to congress between two physically dirty and stinky human beings, or to particular sex acts that involve smelly bodily fluids.

But 'skunk' is not always a negatively loaded term. 'Skunk hair' neutrally describes either deliberate or accidental two-toned black-and-white hair. Skunk-related place names in the United States include Polecat, Tennessee; Polecat Landing, South Carolina; and Polecat Crossing, Wisconsin. Skunk Hollow was the colloquial name of a nineteenth-century free black community settled in New Jersey 60 years before the Thirteenth Amendment abolished slavery.[18]

Equally intriguing is the skunk's linguistic connection in naming the major u.s. city Chicago, as extolled in Carl Sandburg's poem 'Windy City':

Skunk cabbage (*Lysichiton* spp.) gives off a strong odour that can both attract and repel.

Early the red men gave a name to the river,
the place of the skunk,
the river of the wild onion smell,
Shee-caw-go.[19]

The Skunk Hollow historical marker for a rare, 19th-century 'free black community' along the New York/New Jersey border. Black families who lived there called it 'the mountain'; white residents referred to it as 'Skunk Hollow'.

According to Algonquian and Uto-Aztecan linguist Michael McCafferty, '"Chicago" is a French spelling that represents *Šakaakwa*, the word for the striped skunk (*Mephitis mephitis*) in Miami-Illinois, an eastern Great Lakes Algonquian language.'[20]

Often humorous and poetic, terms of venery, which are designations for a group of a particular animal species, offer both the playful 'stench of skunks', in keeping with a 'plague of locusts'

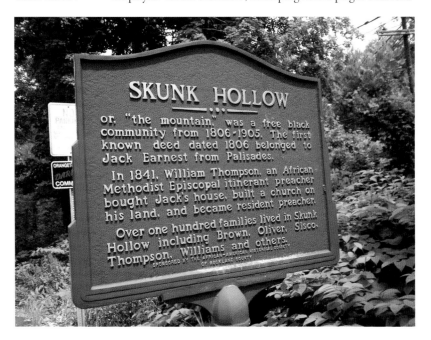

and an 'exaltation of larks', as well as a 'surfeit of skunks', with the additional pleasures of alliteration.

The popular expression 'drunk as a skunk', or the lesser-known 'skunk drunk', shows up in various forms as a colourful synonym for 'wasted', 'smashed', 'blitzed' or, as the British or Australians might say, 'pissed as a newt'. Historically, the phrase 'drunk as . . .' initiates a number of similes in English that include centuries-old variations like 'fiddler', 'fiddler's bitch', a 'lord' or 'a coot'. Chaucer gave us 'We faren as he that dronke is as a moues' (we act like one who is drunk as a mouse) from 'The Knight's Tale'.[21] Theories abound as to the origins of 'drunk as a skunk'. Some swear that any Appalachian moonshiner who has ever pulled a drowned skunk from the corn mash used to make whiskey in a backwoods still would recognize the origin of the phrase. Others speculate that the idiom simply relies on the easy end rhyme. Though it is unclear

The famous Engine #45, known as the 'Super Skunk', a 1924 Baldwin 2-8-2 Mikado Steam Locomotive. It still operates as an entertainment passenger train along the northern Mendocino County California coast.

how popular the use is, the French have their own version, 'pompette comme une moufette', which relies on an amusing rhyme, though a very old expression from the French-speakers in Louisiana, 'saoul comme un grive', translates into English as 'drunk as a thrush'.

The proverb 'Let everyone drown his own skunk' generally means that people are responsible for their own work or choices; one should not expect others to handle one's own dirty work, since drowning a skunk is not a particularly pleasant task.

The association with smell that plagues the linguistic skunk is evident in the name of the Myakka skunk ape, also known as 'the stink ape', a hominid cryptid and mysterious anthropoid that witnesses claim to have repeatedly encountered and even photographed. Now relegated to the category of mythical figure, not unlike the Pacific Northwest Sasquatch, the Nepalese Yeti and the Aboriginal Yowie, the skunk ape is sometimes referred to as the Florida Bigfoot because of its preference for the swamps there. The skunk ape has been described as covered in black fur and possessing glowing red eyes. Of course, its most distinctive feature is the disgusting and unforgettable skunk-like odour emanating from it. The skunk ape has been discredited by experts as either a misidentified orangutan on the loose, or simply a hoax, but in any case, the legend of the Skunk Ape persists. In *Skunk Ape Semester* (2012), a novel by Mike Robinson, researcher Jeremy Fishleder leads a group of college students on a road trip in search of cryptids, including the Skunk Ape, whom Fishleder recalls from a childhood experience:

> The smell, which Mom described as 'like a rancid skunk', returned only in brief and isolated pockets, a sort of noxious ghost sweeping through, an odorous hit and run. It never stayed as long as Mom described it that one night, and, so far as I could tell, it was never as strong.[22]

The origins of the Latin *mephitis* hark back to the pre-Roman goddess of offensive odours. The deified Mefitis was apparently worshipped in cults at Potentia in Transpadane Gaul and particularly in central Italy, where reference can be found to a grove of Mefitis, as well as to a temple in Rome. The fourth-century Roman grammarian and teacher Maurus Servius Honoratus, who authored commentaries on Virgil, describes Mefitis as

> an offensive gas arising from the earth, originating in sulphurous waters; and is of heavier quality in groves, on account of the density of the wooded growth . . . We know, moreover, that such a gas arises only from the corruption of the air . . . So that Mefitis is the goddess of a most offensive odour.[23]

This cribbage board features Muggins the skunk and the potential trouncing of an opponent.

Odour seems to follow skunks wherever they go. *Spilogale putorius* (Eastern spotted skunk) means 'stinky spotted weasel'.

In the French language, the 'striped skunk' (*M. mephitis*) is known as a *moufette rayée*. The Latin taxonomy of skunks owes a debt to the French zoologist, Charles-Lucien Bonaparte, a nephew of the Emperor Napoleon I.

But the 'stink' in skunk is not limited to Romance languages. The Chinese characterize 'skunk' as 臭鼬, chòu yòu. The first character 臭, chòu, equals 'stinky', as in the famous Chinese dish 'stinky tofu' (臭豆腐, chòu dòufu), made of fermented bean curd. The second character of 臭鼬, yòu, refers to ferrets and similar creatures often aligned with the skunk.[24]

The British connection with skunks continues with the card game cribbage, an offspring of the game 'noddy', allegedly invented by English poet Sir John Suckling. The game includes a wooden cribbage board consisting of holes and pegs, and a distinctive scoring system that makes various uses of the word 'skunk'. The 'skunk line', as it is known, is located between holes 90 and 91 of the cribbage board. To cross that line is to 'skunk' one's opponent. Crossing the 'double skunk line', located between holes 60 and 61, delivers the equivalent of four wins. The terms 'skunk' and 'double skunk' in cribbage demonstrate different levels of 'trouncing' an opponent, as well as the triumph of the one who 'skunks'. The verb form of 'skunk' has been in common use since 1843.

Skunks again find their way into war, this time the mysterious Cold War world. 'Skunk Works' became the official alias for the once highly secretive and elusively termed 'Advanced Development Programs', an innovative military project attached to the American global aerospace company Lockheed Martin. The carefully chosen crew of engineers and scientists were charged with designing and developing state-of-the-art jets. But an equally intriguing narrative of Cold War politics of the time emerges, and the role of Skunk Works has much to tell us about the history and culture of war politics and competition in general up to the present. In 1943 the U.S. War Department approached Lockheed's chief engineer, Clarence 'Kelly' Johnson, about developing a jet prototype. After the appearance of a powerful German fighter jet, the USAAF commissioned Lockheed to design and build a competitor in six short months. Kelly launched the project in a rented circus tent, with a staff of about 50 engineers and mechanics, located next to a reeking plastics factory 'whose stench', one of the engineers explains, 'kept the curious at bay'.[25] What took shape was the formation of an unorthodox group of engineers and associates known for secrecy, elitism and independence, free of bureaucratic control. Over the following decades they would develop for Lockheed the U-2, ST-71 Blackbird, the F-117 Nighthawk stealth fighter (developed from the *Have Blue*) and the F-22 Raptor.

But whence the name 'Skunk Works'? Originally, it alluded to 'Skonk Works' from the satirical *Li'l Abner* comic strip, brainchild of American cartoonist Al Capp. Capp's stories focused on a community of hill people (pejoratively called 'hillbillies' in parts of the u.s.) in a depressed area called Dogpatch. On the outskirts of Dogpatch lived a backwoods moonshiner, 'Injun Joe', whose 'Kickapoo Joy Juice' was concocted from old shoes and dead skunks and brewed in a stinky still, 'skonk works'. According to Ben Rich, those working in the circus tent likened the stench emanating from the neighbouring plastics factory to Joe's mal-odorous still. One day a designer in Kelly's circus tent jokingly answered the phone with the greeting 'Skonk Works' and received a tongue-lashing from Kelly. But the name stuck and soon everyone joked about smelling the 'skonk'.[26]

The shift in name to 'Skunk Works' was prompted by a copyright objection by Al Capp's publisher in 1960. The Skunk Works logo now appears on everything from T-shirts and caps to the aircraft themselves. Today's Skunk Works has come a long way from a circus tent next to a plastics factory, relocating to an enormous compound in Palmdale, California, where it maintains its reputation for producing groundbreaking aircrafts. But the name lives on. In fact, 'skunk works' has entered the broader lexicon and achieved common noun status in several dictionaries, referring to any small secretive group within a larger organization that functions relatively autonomously without heavy-handed bureaucratic oversight to further innovation and experimentation.[27] Once again, the independent skunk takes shape.

7 Popular Skunk

Back in 1942, American jazz musicians Cab Calloway (1907–1994) and the Cavaliers recorded the lively 'Skunk Song' in which each singer takes turns lamenting that nobody loves him because he's just a lowly skunk. Envious of his successful friends, the Skunk complains that Big Bad Wolf talks only about his Disney money, Felix the Cat is fat and rich, and Mickey the Mouse is riding in his motor car, while he himself is nothing but a 'dirty old skunk'. Calloway's 'Skunk Song' is of particular historic interest because it was recorded as one of the 'soundies' played in restaurants, bars and night clubs on visual jukeboxes trademarked under the name 'Panoram'.[1] 'Soundies' might be considered the black-and-white precursor to the music video. Featuring 16-mm film images synced to audio performances of famous musicians working in various musical genres, 'soundies' still offer some of the best rare footage of significant African American entertainers, not the least of whom is Calloway polishing off 'Skunk Song' in a final flourish of holding off his nose, while humorously concluding, 'I guess I ain't nothin' but a skunk.'[2]

The skunk inspired the famous spirited and percussive instrumental 'Some Skunk Funk' by Randy and Michael Brecker of the funk and fusion duo the Brecker Brothers.[3] The rhythmic, groove-based musical genre known as 'funk' evolved through idioms of 1950s jazz improvisation rooted in the vernacular of

Singer and band leader Cab Calloway, right, who made famous the hit tune 'Skunk Song', is shown here with friends, actress Lena Horne and vaudeville entertainer 'Bojangles', from the film *Stormy Weather*.

Black American music. Popularized by the Godfather of Soul, James Brown, in the 1960s, funk reached its height in the 1970s with early pioneers like the Ohio Players, Bootsy Collins and the Parliaments. 'Funk' exudes a literal meaning of 'strong odour' or 'stink' (often carrying sexual connotations), hence the connection to skunks. Musical 'funk' is often characterized by a hefty bass line and guitar riffs, and powerful brass sections. 'Funk' relies on syncopated rhythms more than melody, with accents placed on weaker beats.

Among jazz musicians, 'funk' referred to a mellow groove but morphed over time to connote a rhythmic musical genre that typically mixes the languages of jazz, soul and R&B, with a gritty, earthy and carnal sound. Around 1900 the cornetist Buddy Bolden, widely considered the father of New Orleans ragtime music, boldly titled an innovative jazzy and rhythmic piece 'Funky Butt'.

Historian Robert Farris Thompson traces the jazz term 'funk' to African etymological roots relating to odour:

> The slang term 'funky' used in black communities originally referred to strong body odor . . . The black nuance seems to derive from the Ki-Kongo *lu-fuki*, 'bad body odor', and is perhaps reinforced by contact with *fumet*, 'aroma of food and wine', in French Louisiana. But the Ki-Kongo word is closer to the jazz word 'funky' in form and meaning, as both jazzmen and Bakongo use 'funky' and *lu-fuki* to praise persons for the integrity of their art, for having 'worked out' to achieve their aims . . . Hence, 'funk' in American jazz parlance can mean earthiness, a return to fundamentals.[4]

'Skunk Funk' is a comical Merry Melody blending musical and sexual pun inserted in the episode 'That's My Baby' of *The Looney Tunes Show* (2011). It showcases some of the best of cartoon skunk Pepé Le Pew's amorous adventures. Strutting his stuff, Pepé boastfully compares his skunk stench to the pungency of a fine Camembert cheese, playing on our human ambivalence over odours we find simultaneously repugnant and attractive. As Pepé presses his affections, backup singers repeat the refrain, 'It is getting funky in here' and 'It is getting skunky in here.'

But skunks aren't just the musical province of funk. A disastrous but not uncommon fate befell the skunk in the unsentimental licks and grotesque lyrics of the 1972 song 'Dead Skunk (In the Middle of the Road)' by American folk singer Loudon Wainwright III. The singer's whimsical distaste is evident in his urging listeners to roll up the car window and hold their noses when they encounter the stench of a dead skunk in the road.[5] Playing on the skunk's stinky reputation, British band Skunk Anansie, characterized by lead vocalist Deborah Anne

Featured in Wainwright's song, this very real dead skunk in the middle of a road portrays the far-too-common fate of skunks that do not view cars as dangerous.

South Skunk
Blues Society
logo honours
the skunk
in music.

Dyer (aka Skin) as a 'clit-rock group', claims to have added 'skunk' to the name for no other reason than to 'make the name nastier'.[6]

In fact, the skunk's musical connections cross many genres. Quebec rock band GrimSkunk acknowledges that the 'Skunk' in the group's name refers to the skunk cannabis, so named for its musky pungency: the band's signature T-shirts are emblazoned with the image of a dour-faced and very buzzed skunk. Two American bands, one punk and one ska, have chosen the name The Skunks, and from the Basque region in France comes a ska punk band called simply Skunk. The moniker 'Atomic Skunk' was adopted by electronic 'ambient' musician Rich Brodsky from the San Francisco Bay area, while 'Papa Skunk' is the musical production pseudonym of 're-mix artist' Dan Scheidt in Denver, Colorado.

Many blues record labels maintain a convention of drawing names from marginalized animals, like Blind Pig, Alligator, Earwig, Fat Possum and the Chicago-based record label Blue Skunk Music. The South Skunk Blues Society in Newton, Iowa, promotes the blues, and Skunk Farm in Greer, South Carolina, hosts two annual music festivals featuring bluegrass, folk and other Americana: the Spring Skunk Music Fest and the Albino Skunk Music Festival, named in tribute to the mostly white skunks that populate the grounds.

In the popular American children's song, 'Little Skunk Hole', the singer discovers the consequences of interfering with a skunk:

Skunk Farm Albino
Skunk Music
Festival poster
celebrates the
'white' skunks
that roam there,
though they are
not technically
albino.

Oh, I stuck my head
In the little skunk's hole
And the little skunk said,
'Well, bless my soul!
Take it out! Take it out!
Take it out! Remove it!'
Oh, I didn't take it out

138

LIVE MUSIC   CAMPING   CRAFT BEER GARDEN   FOOD TRUCKS   KIDDIELAND   CRAFT VENDORS

ALBINO SKUNK
MUSIC FESTIVAL

SKUNKLANDIA

Tour de Skunk

at the SkunkFarm
GREER, SC

OCTOBER 3, 4, 5, 2013

Lake Street Dive ❀ **Chatham County Line**
Kopecky Family Band ❀ **The Ragbirds**
Lonesome River Band ❀ **Sons of Bill**
Yarn ❀ **Frank Solivan and Dirty Kitchen**
Mountain Standard Time ❀ **Seven Handle Circus**
Underhill Rose ❀ **The Stray Birds** ❀ **Fruition**
The Deadfields ❀ DejaBlue Grass Band ❀ Locust Honey
DB Rielly ❀ The Fox Fire ❀ Tonight's Noise ❀ Darby Wilcox

WNCW 88.7   edible UPCOUNTRY   fête   ROCK

WWW.ALBINOSKUNK.COM

The cover of David T. Greenberg's beloved children's book *Skunks!* (2001).

And the little skunk said
'If you don't take it out,
You'll wish you were dead.
Take it out! Take it out!'
Pheew! I removed it.

The stinky skunk figures in young children's literature as well, for example in *Pee-U, I Think There is a Skunk in Our School*. A comical mix-up over the odour of the plant skunkweed sitting on the teacher's desk leads to the discovery of a skunk family living much too close for comfort. In hilarious rhyming quatrains the narrator of David T. Greenberg's *Skunks!* enumerates the advantages of skunks, including 'Get married to a skunk / And save a thousand bucks / He can carbonate all the wedding drinks / And won't require a tux'. The book ends with 'you may rest content / With your loving skunk companions / Who are truly heaven-scent'.[7]

But the skunk often symbolizes the misunderstood social outcast. There is almost nothing worse than 'smelling bad', and the elision between body odour and social status starts early in childhood. Object lessons on tolerance and acceptance mirror contemporary discourses of difference, diversity and inclusion.

'Helping Children Learn Tolerance' is the subtitle of the picture book *There's a Skunk in My Bunk*, written by a licensed clinical psychologist. Upon discovering a skunk in his bed one night, Timmy initially responds with disgust. Only when the patient skunk explains that he doesn't stink at all does Timmy learn that 'That famous strong scent for which I am known / Protects me, so enemies leave me alone'. The book concludes: 'Think for yourself and do not quickly judge others / For the truth is all creatures are sisters and brothers.'[8]

This lesson is echoed in *It's What's Inside that Counts*, when squirrel Justin befriends skunk Gregory, even after all the other 'deep woods' squirrel friends have fled. But Justin does 'a very kind and brave thing' by embracing Gregory in a full-on hug, proving that skunks don't spray automatically or without reason. Over the next few days, the two 'became the best of friends'. Newly enlightened, Justin teaches his other squirrel friends to accept Gregory. 'He may be different on the outside', Justin explains, 'but on the inside he's very kind and wonderful. I'm sure you'd like him if you got to know him.' Not so readily

A 1980s Mexican sugar figurine of Little Red Riding Hood alters the traditional story by including a (damaged) skunk instead of the wolf.

convinced, the other squirrels shun Gregory until he discovers a cure for a contagious virus, 'squirrel fever'. By the end, Gregory is guest of honour at the squirrels' picnic and the squirrels admit that 'it doesn't matter what's on the outside, it's what on the inside that really counts'.[9]

A dark, wet night brings a number of different animal guests to the door of the wee fat man and the wee fat woman in *Is There Room on the Feather Bed*? The animals are cuddled together, but when wee fat woman ushers in the skunk, the wee fat man and other animals flee outside, preferring the 'dark wet night' to sharing a bed with a skunk. Only after it dawns on the scattered animals that while they shiver outside the skunk is cosily curled up inside do they decide to return and share the warmth of the house. 'So come back inside', says the wee fat woman, 'Let's all be friends. We'll have breakfast in bed until the rain ends.'[10]

The skunk also teaches self-acceptance, as the titular protagonist of the comic strip series *Ramone Cologne: Skunk's Tale* invariably demonstrates, as he seeks to be loved for himself. In Audrey Penn's children's book *Sassafras,* the eponymous skunk learns that 'what makes him different is what makes him special'. Plagued by self-loathing, Sassafras comes to realize he can protect his forest friends by spraying to alert them all to an intruder. Earning their respect and gratitude, Sassafras concludes that 'we are who we are. That's the way it should be. Even smelly-old, stinky-old, funky-old me!'[11]

Like Sassafras, skunk Fuzzle in *New Kid in Town* struggles with ostracization by the other animals in Pleasant Woods. Porcupine Cuddles asks if Fuzzle has any special skills, pointing to his own needles as an example that 'Creator of all things' has endowed each animal with various forms of protection. Having sent a coyote running in the opposite direction, Fuzzle realizes 'that if the Maker had given me the special strong scent that had chased off the coyote, and had made me with this special defensive ability, then I [sh]ould no longer feel shame and embarrassment concerning it'.[12]

But in *Skunk's Spring Surprise*, when protagonist Skunk awakens from her winter nap to discover all her friends missing, she jumps to conclusions: 'Perhaps they hate the way I smell', and she

The much-feared back end of a skunk, which also offers the opportunity to view the beauty of the fanned black-and-white tail.

'stamps her feet and starts to yell'. To her surprise, the forest friends are off planning a surprise party for her.[13]

The helper skunk is depicted in *The Berenstain Bears and the Neighborly Skunk*, when Mr Skunk proves he is a 'pleasant, friendly little fellow despite his "strong" reputation' and wins everyone's admiration after delivering a 'short burst of his "strength"' to the nostrils of the bullying Too-tall Grizzly, who has been tormenting the skunk's new friends.[14] In a slightly different register, the helper skunk in *Jonathan Michael and the Uninvited Guest* proves her usefulness to a farmer by eating harmful pests.

The skunk-human bond is developed in *Summer of the Skunks* after ten-year-old Jill's family rescue a nest of baby skunks and adopt one they name Rabies, whom they de-scent. Rabies is beloved by Jill's older sister Margo. However, commensurate with a common young adult literary tradition of sacrificing wild animal companions for the personal growth of human characters, Rabies tragically dies only to be replaced by a kitten, suggesting a return to the natural order of domestic life.

Perhaps best known as Pepé Le Pew's creator, Chuck Jones developed another skunk character in his illustrated children's book *William the Backwards Skunk*. William's stripe mistakenly runs down his underside, making it difficult for other animals to know he is a skunk until it is 'too late'. A clever plan is hatched among all the prey animals to paint generic Acme Skunk Stripes down their own backs. All the predators take off, and the book concludes, 'And nobody ever ate anybody again – at least not in *that* part of the forest.'[15]

Associating skunks with a peculiarly provincial idea of 'Frenchness' takes stinkiness and sexiness to a whole new level. Miz Mam'selle Hepzibah, the warm-hearted, coy French skunk character in the highly popular *Pogo* comic strip, was actually modelled on the real-life mistress and eventual wife of the creator, Walt Kelly. But unlike Pepé, Hepzibah does not do the lusting, but is lusted after by almost every male character in the strip. The name of the amiable animated skunk Odie O. Cologne puns on the French perfume eau de cologne, created in the early eighteenth century in Cologne, Germany, by an Italian scent mixer, Giovanni Maria Farina, who originally named it *Kölnisch Wasser*, and which became popular in the royal houses of Europe. The original formula is still produced by Farina Gegenüber in Cologne, but many other firms have used the name 'eau de cologne', including Roger & Gallet, which purchased the rights in the mid-nineteenth century by buying a Paris perfumery business founded by a member of the Farina family.

Probably the most famous and beloved of aromatic animated skunks is the 'hyper-French' and hopelessly romantic self-styled ladies' man Pepé Le Pew, who presses his unwanted affections on various female characters including the long-suffering Penelope Pussycat, who fails to repel his attentions. Le Pew remains ardently convinced that, despite being a cat, her black-and-white markings make her a luscious female skunk. Though treated comically, the Le Pew series plays with our divided relationship to the sexualized and odiferous body. Double entendres abound, not the least of which is the play on 'perfume'. In *Really Scent* Pepé muses, 'I must find out what this "pew" means every time I appear', and proceeds to consult a dictionary. Upon discovering the truth, he cries out: 'No, no, not me! . . . C'est impossible pew, non.'[16]

A more recent addition to the French skunk cartoon pantheon is Fifi La Fume, a hyper-feminine purple-and-white skunk sporting a pink bow in her hair, appearing in Warner Brothers' *Tiny Toon Adventures*. Like Pepé, Fifi also fixates on a put-upon cat, in this case, one named Furrball. But unlike Pepé, her malodorous scent is not constant, waxing and waning with her affections, still making love a stinky business.

While the original Felix Salten *Bambi* books did not include the skunk Flower, he became an embellishment of the Walt Disney animated feature. Naive fawn Bambi, out sniffing in an aromatic meadow, finds himself nose to nose with a black-and-white striped skunk but mistakes him for a flower. His sweet-scented moniker for the skunk causes rabbit friend Thumper to roll backwards in

hysterical laughter. Another addition to the cast of cartoon skunks is the sassy Stella, voiced in the animated feature *Over the Hedge* (2006) by American comedian Wanda Sykes.

But a more serious side to skunks emerges in literary poetry, where they symbolize beauty, sexuality, existential dread and human longing. The melancholy speaker in Robert Lowell's famous poem 'Skunk Hour' addresses the alienation he feels in a changing social and economic landscape on Nautilus Island, Maine, and illuminates the loss of a culture and a decaying social structure. He confesses, 'My mind's not right', and at his most desperate the speaker admits, 'I myself am hell; nobody's here – only skunks, that search / in the moonlight for a bite to eat.'[17] The dash following the word 'here' invites the reader to consider the emptiness of the speaker's world as he stands on his back steps and views the startling image of the moonlit mother skunk and her kits moving down the street, foraging for food in the garbage of humanity.

The optimistic and oblivious 'French' Pepé Le Pew and his never-ending pursuit of unrequited *l'amour*.

147

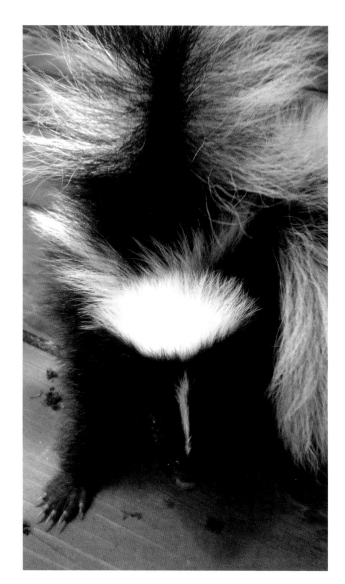

Close-up portraying the sensual beauty of a young skunk's face celebrated in Nye's poem 'Valentine for Ernest Mann'.

'Skunk Hour' is a reply to 'The Armadillo', written by Lowell's poet friend Elizabeth Bishop and dedicated to him. Though liminal animals, the skunk and armadillo become transcendent through the beauty of lyrics and imagination. Bishop's armadillo represents the vulnerable natural world, while Lowell's skunk represents the power and freedom of a natural world refusing to alter its habits to accommodate a changing, anthropocentric world. Lowell's description of his skunks walking plantigrade, their white stripes and glowing 'moonstruck eyes', renders them magical. There is beauty in the mother skunk's 'ostrich tail', as she scavenges a cast-off sour cream cup. The fierce determination of the foraging mother skunk who draws sustenance from human refuse offers hope to Lowell's tormented speaker.

One might not expect a skunk to symbolize romantic love, but that is exactly what happens in Naomi Shihab Nye's poem, 'Valentine for Ernest Mann'. Avoiding clichéd expressions of love, the speaker reports,

> Once I knew a man who gave his wife
> two skunks for a valentine.
> He couldn't understand why she was crying.
> 'I thought they had such beautiful eyes.'[18]

The two skunks stand in sharp contrast to the more familiar romantic images like red roses and hearts. Acknowledging the inadequacies of language, the speaker abandons metaphor altogether, for the gift of actual skunks is a particular and refreshing gesture of love.

In a very sexy poem, 'The Skunk,' Irish poet Seamus Heaney's speaker yearns for his long-absent wife, for whom he still feels intense sexual passion. Writing love letters, he finds himself anticipating the regular nightly visits from a female skunk who serves as both muse and figure of desire; she has both an aura of ordinariness and a mysterious allure.[19] Like Nye's skunks, Heaney's ordinary but sensual skunk, in all her animality, embodies the speaker's sexual and emotional desire, triggering memories and erotic longing. As he recalls waiting while his wife performed her bedtime rituals, skunk and wife merge in her 'head-down, tail-up hunt in a bottom drawer / For the black plungeline nightdress.'[20]

For all three poets, the skunk carries spiritual weight. Heaney compares the black-striped skunk to a chasuble at a funeral; Lowell's nocturnal skunk band arrives on Main Street 'under the chalk-dry and spar spire of the Trinitarian Church'. And for Nye, a poem, with its own stamp of spiritual renewal, can't be ordered up 'like you order a taco'. Poems, for Nye, like love and desire, and even the skunk, are mysterious and elusive.

In one of the more bizarre twists on literary skunks, American science fiction writer Clifford Simak makes skunks the heroes of his fantastical alien invasion novel *They Walked like Men* (1979). Though the title refers to space aliens who resemble bowling balls but are also able to shape-shift into human form, the fact is skunks do literally walk like men (and all humans) – flat-footed. Known for outlandish plots, Simak spins a mephitic yarn featuring clever, malevolent aliens, who are up to no good, buying all the property on earth to develop an interstellar resort, and annihilate the human race.

Lady with an Ermine, Leonardo da Vinci, 1489–90, oil on panel. As evocative as it is mysterious, some believe this odd animal could easily be the artist's imagining of a ferret or a skunk.

Parker Graves, an alert reporter, catches wind of the insidious cosmic realtor plot and sets out to warn the world. But he is unsuccessful in convincing anyone else of the threat because, ironically, the aliens operate according to human property laws. How can Graves prove danger before it's too late? Lo and behold, he discovers their passion for the smell of skunk spray. Graves hatches a plan unlikely to be seen again in the annals of sci-fi. For help, he turns to an old skunk farmer he learns about from a fellow

reporter, and who lives with and raises skunks for pets. In one of many impossible twists, Graves convinces the farmer to drive a truckload of spraying skunks into the centre of town. As alien bowling balls roll through the streets drawn by the irresistible smell, Graves exposes their evil plot en masse to the public. In the nick of time, plot foiled, skunks save the planet.

Aliens are not the only literary characters seduced by the skunk's powerful musk. Justin Courter's quirky narrator, Damien Youngquist, of the wild, satirical romp *Skunk: A Love Story*, obsessively fetishizes skunk musk, which he calls 'the richest of all olfactory pleasures . . . a bittersweet combination of lilac, tilled earth, MacDougal's beer, dogwood blossoms, apple pie, fresh snow, and Moschus – the miniature Himalayan musk deer'.[21] His fetid fixation leads to acquiring skunks of his own in order to indulge his habit any time he wishes, by holding a skunk over his head and squirting a stream of musk spray directly into his mouth, or drinking harvested musk from a jar. Though quickly alienated by a narrow-minded community, he serendipitously meets marine biologist Pearl, whose erotic delight in fish smells creates a sensual and emotional bond between the two. A social outcast, Damien eventually retreats into a hermitic life on a farm he shares with his ever-expanding skunk family. As a deterrent to nosy neighbours, he borders his field with a hedge of the equally redolent skunk cabbage. However, his solitude is interrupted by a cast of characters that include a bullying marijuana grower and members of an animal rights organization, SAFETY. A web of tense and violent conflicts results in the murder of one of his favourite skunks, Father. When skunk spray becomes a profitable drug, SS, he is prosecuted in court for posing a danger to society. But Damien's legal troubles are the least of his worries. His excessive consumption of skunk musk ultimately leads to blindness. In jail, Damien endures the nightmare of a hallucinogenic and mind-altering withdrawal from his fetid habit. Ordered into a psychiatric hospital, Damien undergoes extensive treatment for skunk addiction. When Pearl reappears to bring him home, she presents him with an ultimatum: 'it's going to be me or the musk. You can't have both.'[22] Damien shakily chooses Pearl. The novel ends with the blind Damien groping his way through the farmhouse he shares with Pearl and their infant son, resigned to a new life. But the breeze wafting through his open window conjures up not only luscious scents of earth and plants, but the alluring skunk smell. It's easy to imagine that Damien is not yet done with his skunky business.

Skunk spray jokes occupy an established place in the pantheon of scatological humour, right up there with defecation and flatulence. *Furry Vengeance*, an eco-friendly film of 2010 that was so bad that NPR reviewer Mark Jenkins titled his review 'Furry Vengeance: Skunks Aren't All that Stink', features a number of revenge moments, among them the infamous skunk spray scene.[23] Midwesterner Dan Sanders, played by Brendan Fraser, relocates his family to Oregon to oversee a housing development project that threatens surrounding wild forest lands. The animals band together in revolt and seek revenge on Dan and his boss. With a mastermind raccoon in charge of meting out Dan's justice, viewers are treated to the spectacle of a helpless, gasping Dan trapped in his car while angry skunks fill the confined space with spray.

The familiar 'trapped with a skunk' scenario recurs in an episode of the American reality television show, *Billy the Exterminator*, featuring a skunk in an airplane hangar, wreaking havoc on humans. Writers of the 1960s American television sitcom *Gomer Pyle, U.S.M.C.* couldn't resist their own skunk spray episode. Goofy Gomer, a lowly private in the U.S. Marines and lovable backwoods anti-hero, befriends a skunk he names Private Ralph. Much of the humour in the episode is drawn from bumpkin Gomer's attachment to the stinky animal. To the annoyance of Gomer's perpetually outraged antagonist Sergeant Carter, Private Ralph is discovered and immediately banned from the platoon base. However, Gomer is ever the 'wise fool', and when he helps Carter defeat a rival sergeant in a barrack inspection by letting Ralph loose in the vicinity, Gomer and Ralph the skunk save the day: 'That's one skunk that really earned his stripes.'

A welcoming skunk serves as a mascot for the annual Mephit Furmeet 'furry' convention held in Memphis, Tennessee, and appears in their logo wearing a polka-dotted party hat and holding balloons. There are probably as many definitions of 'furry' as there are people involved in the subculture. Most 'furries', or 'furs', share strong interests in and identification with anthropomorphic animals with human personalities. The expression of

Sexy skunk crawling costume demonstrates playful associations of odiferous skunks with eros and sex.

these attractions takes many forms that may include drawing animals, designing avatars and cartoons and, for a small minority, dressing up in animal costumes called fursuits or partial suits, and even role playing by assuming a furry persona (a 'fursona'), often with like-minded furries. Furry conventions bring together those also interested in animal art and cartooning, many claiming strong emotional and spiritual connections to animals.

Because prurient themes appeal, media coverage has focused on sensationalized portrayals of furry culture as a sexual tendency (zoophilia or plushophilia), ignoring the majority of furries who identify so strongly with a particular animal that the connection takes on a deeply transcendent quality.

One aspect of furry culture is designing and building one's own fursuit, though not all furry fans wear fursuits. Those in a fashion pinch can turn to prêt-à-porter for tails, ears, hats, hoodies and other animal accessories.

One of the most famous furry comics stars is 'skunkette' Sabrina, from the webcomic *Sabrina Online*, a favourite with many in the furry fandom.[24] Introduced in 1996 by creator and artist Eric W. Schwartz, Sabrina is drawn as a sexy-nerd anthropomorphic skunk with glasses. She works as a computer geek and website designer, and much of the storyline addresses life in the virtual and online worlds. Produced quarterly, the strip focuses on the vicissitudes of Sabrina's quotidian social and love life, including characters like the raccoon R. C., who is shyly attracted to Sabrina, her skunk boss ZigZag (whose grandfather was a white tiger) and a various assortment of anthropomorphic animals like Thomas, a grey wolf; squirrels; and even a squirrel-wolf hybrid. *Sabrina Online* has garnered an enthusiastic fandom all over the world and has been translated into eight languages, including Polish, Spanish, Russian, German and Danish.

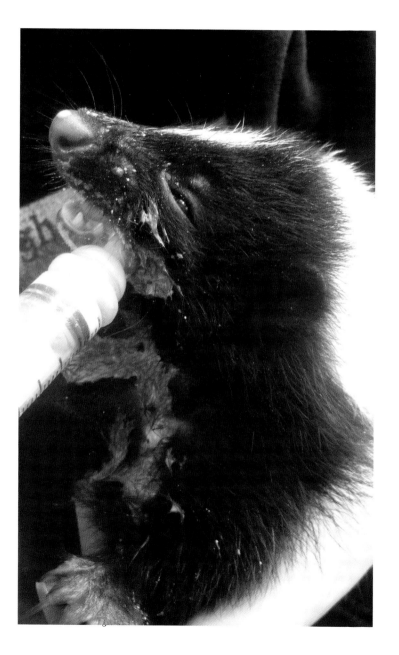

8 Skunk Sanctuary

Nowhere is the paradox of the skunk's dual role as both wild and domestic better illustrated than in the world of rescue. Simply put, we protect and save animals we value aesthetically, economically and emotionally. Even within the same species, lives of individuals are often valued differently. Skunks raised and slaughtered on fur farms are dispensable commodities, whereas a fur farm skunk sold as an animal companion may end up a treasured family member. Similarly, a wild mother skunk denning in the window well of a house is viewed as a nuisance and shot to death, but her orphaned kits may be saved and transported to a wildlife rescue organization. Our willingness to sacrifice some for food, fashion and entertainment stands in direct contrast to those, even of the same species, that we save, protect and even love.

Human actions have very material consequences for skunks. And there are often times when skunks need our help. Two different types of rescue organizations can help meet that need. The first caters to abandoned or injured wildlife, with the main goal to rehabilitate and reintroduce wild animals back into natural environments. The second focuses on saving abandoned or owner-surrendered pet skunks. Since domesticated skunks lack skills necessary to survive on their own, the lucky ones end up in safe havens. Some North American non-profit wildlife rescue organizations, like Dove Key Ranch in Texas,

Hungry orphaned baby skunk being bottle-fed by a licensed wildlife rehabilitator in Bloomington, Indiana.

specialize in skunk rehabilitation, working to 'promote a humane coexistence between humans and their wildlife neighbors.'[1]

Most animal shelters, some funded by cities or counties, or private monies, are already overwhelmed by the millions of unwanted cats and dogs surrendered each year, and most are not legally permitted to take skunks or other wild animals. The fantasy of skunk ownership is not easily reconciled with the challenging realities that put exotic pets like skunks in real jeopardy.

Whereas pet-skunk rescuers work to socialize and match skunks to new human caretakers, licensed wildlife rehabilitators deliberately minimize contact between humans and skunks to very essential acts of care, like bottle-feeding or cleaning. With rescued kits, rehabilitators mimic the mother's role, but as kits mature, contact with humans significantly decreases. Wild skunks that end up in legitimate rescues must never become acclimated to humans, tempting though it is to fall in love with a skunk. Whether orphaned or injured, wild skunks undergoing rehabilitation are prepared for eventual release through a process known as 'wilding up'. This often involves placing the animals in outside enclosures and encouraging them to learn the survival skills they will need, like foraging for food.[2]

The common denominator in both pet skunk and wildlife rescue is a story of human interference and human intervention, creating yet another dichotomy involving our black-and-white friend.

Skunkfest is a lively annual festival held at a park in North Ridgeville, Ohio, celebrating responsible pet-skunk ownership with a day devoted to educational games, activities and contests. Skunkfest is a fundraiser for the non-profit rescue Skunk Haven, billed by its intrepid skunk-loving operator Deborah Cipriani as 'an international rescue and assistance group' offering assistance

and education to pet-skunk owners, and those unable to keep their pet skunks any longer. With a focus on proper health care and enrichment, various events on the day I attended rewarded skunk owners for their pets' beauty, health and well-being. A knowledgeable veterinarian was on hand to act as judge and educational consultant.

A pet chocolate-chip-coloured skunk undergoes a weight and health check at Skunk Fest.

In her daily life, Cipriani devotes tremendous energies to the many skunks who share her home. Her day begins at 4.30 a.m. every morning to feed her charges and clean their boxes. Juggling a full-time job outside the home, she heads to work at 9 a.m. and returns home at 7.30 p.m., to begin the process all over again. Hers is the only skunk rescue in the u.s. licensed for both pet skunks and wild skunks. Since it is illegal to keep wild skunks, a wild skunk unequipped to return to the wilds, often because of injury, must either be euthanized or find work as an animal ambassador in humane education, a service for which Cipriani is licensed. A committed skunk advocate, Cipriani's mission is to inform and counter misinformation with facts.[3]

The Florida Skunk Rescue is a loosely linked network of licensed skunk owners who temporarily foster unwanted pet skunks until appropriate homes can be found. They sponsor the

A pet champagne-coloured skunk is evaluated by a professional judge during a Skunk Fest contest.

annual National Skunk Show in Florida, with a similar focus on proper care and health. The Florida Skunk Rescue vows that foster skunks will not be caged, except for transport, and will live in foster homes where they are welcome to sleep alongside human companions in bed. Legitimate skunk rescues follow careful protocols to ensure new homes are a good match, perhaps charging small adoption fees to offset care costs. While pet skunks are surrendered for various reasons, including biting, mischief or owner allergies, the underlying reason is almost always that prospective owners failed to do adequate research.

Internationally recognized expert in skunky matters Dr Jerry Dragoo, a researcher in the biology department at the University of New Mexico and self-described mephitologist, discourages pet-skunk ownership. His Institute for the Betterment of Skunks and Skunk Reputations provides an extensive resource of evolutionary and natural history, as well as loads of skunk facts. His published research contributed significantly to scientific skunk literature, not the least of which is his co-authored paper solidifying the skunk's taxonomic family move from Mustelidae to Mephitidae, discussed in chapter One.[4] Advantageous to his role as skunk researcher and rescuer is his limited sense of smell and relative indifference to the spray.

Skunk ownership flourishes in countries without native skunks. Great Britain recently held the second annual Exotic Pet Awareness Day just south of Birmingham. Events are modelled after dog and cat shows, with categories like Best Male and Best Female Skunk, and Best in Show. Prizes are awarded for 'most impressive tail, temperament, and cutest nose'.[5] On the continent, organizations devoted to skunks are popping up, like the Dutch Skunk Foundation, dedicated to the rescue and welfare of surrendered pet skunks. The Dutch Skunk Foundation cautions those considering a pet skunk: 'Keeping a skunk is not as easy as it seems.'[6]

Human development and diminishing habitat negatively affect native animals, encouraging an escalating presence of urban and suburban wildlife. The adaptable qualities of skunks increase the likelihood of more human–skunk encounters. However, most humans are not as flexible as skunks and not as willing to coexist, and the view that urban wildlife is a nuisance may lead either to removal or, worse, extirpation.

Those who believe the wild 'exists out there, not here' expect animals to stay outside the human-drawn borders of property lines. But humans have inadvertently made urban and suburban spaces attractive to wildlife, through well-fertilized lawns and edible ornamental plants, outside pet food, careless disposal of garbage and open compost heaps. Such attractants can be easily modified or eliminated, but misinformation about skunks in particular, and suspicion of residential wildlife in general, mean skunks remain at risk from humans.

In addition to stinky reputations, skunks fight a bad rap as a primary vector of the rabies virus throughout North America. While rabies infection is certainly serious, it may come as a surprise that, according to the Centers for Disease Control and Prevention, rabies-related human fatalities in the u.s. average roughly one to three a year. Ninety-nine per cent of all human rabies cases in the world, around 50,000, occur in poor and resource-starved areas of Asia and Africa, where unvaccinated dogs are the major source of infection.[7] Human fatalities from wild host animals like foxes, skunks and raccoons are very rare.[8] Rabies is often transmitted through saliva via bites or deep scratches but does not penetrate unbroken skin. When skunks or other animals are infected, they are not only carriers but ultimately victims of the disease. Any animal with clinical signs of rabies will die within a week or so. Controversy persists over whether skunks are more likely to spread rabies than fellow wildlife; an argument for decreased likelihood

is their well-advertised defence for avoiding close encounters, which reduces opportunities for transmission. Rabies transmission among wild skunks themselves is believed to increase during the heightened aggression associated with the mating season, and the practice of communal denning. Dragoo reminds us that rabies 'is a disease that should be respected, but not feared. There is a preventative that is virtually 100% effective if applied prior to the onset of rabies symptoms.'[9]

High skunk mortality statistics demonstrate that human beings are actually far more dangerous to skunks than the reverse. Humans are credited with causing the deaths of nearly half of all skunks born every year, through a combination of speeding cars, shootings and poisonings.

The reigning queen of Skunk Fest, held by her proud owner, both crowned with matching tiaras.

Skunk kit siblings enjoy a meal together.

Panicked responses to eliminate skunks have sometimes backfired. A *New York Times* story of mistaken identity from 1884, headlined 'Shot for a Skunk', chronicled a gun-toting farmer who went after the skunk he believed was raiding his chickens but ended up mortally wounding an unnamed man hiding there.[10] In a 1928 report, 'Gunning for Skunk, Man Kills Wife', an armed Kansas homeowner who crawled under his house to shoot a nesting skunk accidentally discharged the gun through the kitchen floor, killing his wife.[11] Such shooting accidents are not just a thing of the past. In 2012 a family Halloween party in Beaver County, Pennsylvania, almost ended tragically when an armed relative tracking a skunk in the yard mistakenly shot and wounded his nine-year-old cousin, who was disguised in a black costume with a white tail.[12]

The Humane Society of the u.s. counsels patience on the part of those living among urban wildlife. A skunk taking up close residence that doesn't involve imminent conflict likely has made a temporary birth den. When the kits mature, the family will exit and exterior access points can be cleaned and sealed up. If a skunk dens inside or under a house, trapping and removal from the house may be necessary, but the animals can be safely released into the same area. Though certainly superior to destruction, relocation should be a last resort. Controversy plagues wildlife relocation; though some wildlife removal specialists may trap and relocate wildlife with good intentions, survival rates of relocated animals are low. Many cannot withstand the stress of transport. Surviving skunks dumped in unfamiliar locales will find themselves disorientated and in stiff competition with established residents for limited resources.

With human fear of skunk spray, it's no surprise that advertisements for wildlife removal services proliferate, some with catchy names like Critter Ridders or Pesky Critters. Focusing on disease and other potential dangers to people, pets, buildings and property, advertising copy often characterizes wildlife as 'menacing' and even alludes to potential attacks on children and companion animals. Pest control company Orkin's slogan, 'Don't let wildlife become a nuisance', is a typical lead-in. Good wildlife relocation companies will first educate owners on humanely discouraging guests and other preventative measures. If relocation is preferred, company reputation, time of year and the nature of the proposed new location should all be carefully considered. An Oklahoma-based company, The Skunk Whisperer, advocates no-trap, no-kill services focusing on education and remediation, a philosophy that integrates prevention and management.

Learning to coexist with skunks and other wildlife has the potential to enrich our daily lives. There is much we can learn by observing and appreciating the animals around us who live their lives out in the open. The presence of urban wildlife affords us a unique opportunity to deepen our understanding. Skunks are physically majestic creatures, with amiable natures and a quiet power. Their patient, live-and-let-live philosophy is a reminder to coexist harmoniously with others. If we take the opportunity, we may help to close the moral gap of arbitrary and inconsistent attitudes towards individual animals, even of the same species, some of which we choose to eat or wear, some we view as nuisances, and some we welcome into our homes and our hearts.

Timeline of the Skunk

40 MILLION MYA (OLIGOCENE)	**34–32 MILLION MYA**	**12–11 MILLION MYA**
Origin of skunk lineage	Skunk family originates	Earliest-known appearance of *Palaeomephitis steinheimensis* in Germany

1839	**1900**	**1900s**
Charles Darwin describes his first encounters with skunks in *The Voyage of the Beagle*	The state of Maine annually produces 25,000 gallons of skunk oil, sold at $4 a gallon	Skunk fur exceeds the trade in muskrat fur (previously the most traded fur)

1974	**2006**
Almost-complete skunk skull and lower jaw of *Martinogale faulli* (Faull's skunk) is found in Red Rock Canyon, California. This is 9 million years old and a new species of ancestral skunk in the Americas	Animal Welfare Act prohibits de-scenting skunks in the UK

| 11–3 MILLION MYA | 1500–1700 | 1800 |

Promephitis is found in Eurasia and in Gansu Province, northern China. *Promephitis* is probably not a direct ancestor of the modern-day Southeast Asian stink badger.

New World explorers refer to skunks in their journals

North American skunk fur is popularly used in trade

| 1940 | 1942 | 1945 |

Post-Depression era U.S. skunk-fur sales rise significantly and pelt prices double

Flower appears as Bambi's skunk friend in the animated feature *Bambi*

Famed amorous cartoon skunk Pepé Le Pew first struts his stuff across the big screen

| 2009 | 2009 |

Prada and Fendi show skunk-fur handbags and accessories in clothing lines

Skunks reclassified as *Mephitis mephitis*

References

INTRODUCTION

1 Rich Olson and Andrea M. Lewis, 'Skunk Ecology and Damage
  Management Techniques for Homeowners' (1999),
  www.wyomingextension.org, accessed 8 December 2014.
2 David Lantz, 'Economic Value of North American Skunks',
  Farmers' Bulletin, 587 (1917), p. 13.
3 The term 'possum' is used broadly and colloquially in the U.S.,
  although it actually refers to antipodean mammals. Though not as
  commonly used, 'opossum' is the formal name for the American
  species.
4 *Is That Skunk?*, film in the PBS documentary series *Nature*
  (25 January 2009).

1 HISTORICAL SKUNK

1 Ernest Thompson Seton, *Wild Animals at Home* (Garden City, NY,
  1913), p. 97.
2 H. E. Anthony, *Mammals of America* (New York, 1917), p. 132.
3 John Lawson, *A New Voyage to Carolina* (Chapel Hill, NC, 1984), p. 124.
4 Miguel de Asúa and Roger French, *A New World of Animals: Early
  Modern Europeans on the Creatures of Iberian America* (Aldershot
  and Burlington, VT, 2005), p. 73.
5 Ibid.
6 Charles Darwin, *A Naturalist's Voyage Around the World* [*Voyage of
  the Beagle*] [1839] (London, 1860), p. 83.

7 See *The Century Dictionary and Cyclopedia*, revd edn (New York, 1914), p. 7043.

8 Gary E. Moulton, ed., *The Definitive Journals of Lewis and Clark*, 7 vols (Lincoln, NE, 2002), entry dated Friday, 28 February 1806.

9 Joel Asaph Allen, 'The Generic Names of the Mephitinae', *Bulletin of the American Museum of Natural History*, XIV (1901), p. 326; Jerry Dragoo, 'Dragoo Institute for the Betterment of Skunks and Skunk Reputations', http://dragoo.org, accessed 8 December 2014.

10 Arthur H. Howell, 'Revision of the Skunks of the Genus Spilogale', *North American Fauna*, no. 26 (Washington, DC, 1906), pp. 5–8.

11 Allen, 'Generic Names of the Mephitinae', pp. 332–3.

12 Ibid., p. 325.

13 Ibid., p. 333.

14 Ibid.

15 J. R. Boisserie, F. Lihoreau and M. Brunet, 'The Position of Hippopotamidae within Cetartiodactyla', *Proceedings of the National Academy of Sciences of the USA*, CII/5 (2005), pp. 1537–41.

2 SKUNKS IN NOT SO BLACK AND WHITE

1 J. W. Dragoo and R. L. Honeycutt, 'Systematics of Mustelid-like Carnivores', *Journal of Mammalogy*, LXVIII (1997), pp. 426–43.

2 M. I. Schiaffini, et al., 'Taxonomic Status of Southern South American *Conepatus* (Carnivora: Mephitidae)', *Zoological Journal of the Linnaean Society*, CLXVII (2013), pp. 327–44.

3 Jerry Dragoo, 'Dragoo Institute for the Betterment of Skunks and Skunk Reputations', http://dragoo.org, accessed 8 December 2014.

4 Relied on were Spanish dictionaries, as well as email exchanges with Indiana University biology reference librarian Roger Beckman, English professor Alberto Varon and Spanish professor Manuel Diaz. Other parts of Latin America use regional terms for 'skunk', including *mapurite* in Venezuela.

5 Juan Ignacio Molina, *The Geographical, Natural and Civil History of Chili*, [trans. R. Alsop], 2 vols (Middletown, CT, 1808), p. 203.

6 X. Wang, D. P. Whistler and G. T. Takeuchi, 'A New Basal Skunk *Martinogale* (Carnivora, Mephitinae) from Late Miocene Dove Spring Formation, California and Origin of New World mephitines', *Journal of Vertebrate Paleontology*, xxv/4 (2005), pp. 936–49.

3 ESSENCE OF SKUNK

1 Ernest Thompson Seton, 'The Well Meaning Skunk', in *Wild Animals at Home* (Garden City, NY, 1913), pp. 95–108.

2 Charles Darwin, *Journal of Research into the Geology and Natural History of the Various Counties Visited by HMS 'Beagle'* (London, 1839), entry for 23 August 1833.

3 Juan Ignacio Molina, *The Geographical, Natural and Civil History of Chili*, [trans. R. Alsop], 2 vols (Middletown, CT, 1808), p. 203.

4 Diane Ackerman, 'Smell', in *A Natural History of the Senses* (New York, 1991), p. 12.

5 D. Michael Stoddard, *The Scented Ape: The Biology and Culture of Human Odour* (Cambridge, 1990), p. 163.

6 Ted Andrews, *Animal Speak: The Spiritual and Magical Powers of Creatures Great and Small* (St Paul, MN, 2000), p. 313.

7 Edmond de Goncourt, *Chérie* (Paris, 1884), pp. 300–302.

8 Havelock Ellis, *Sexual Selection in Man* (Philadelphia, PA, 1905), pp. 97–9.

9 Josh Howgego, 'Sense for Scents Traced Down to Genes', www.nature.com, 1 August 2013.

10 'For Scent-imental Reasons', *Looney Tunes*, dir. Chuck Jones (Warner Brothers, 1949).

11 Ackerman, 'Smell', p. 12.

12 Adam Hadhazy, 'Do Pheromones Play A Role in Our Sex Lives?', www.scientificamerican.com, 13 February 2012.

13 Joe Palca, *Annoying: The Science of What Bugs Us* (Hoboken, NJ, 2011), p. 61.

14 William F. Wood, 'The History of Skunk Defensive Secretion Research', *Chemical Educator*, IV/2 (1999), pp. 44–50.

15 Ibid.

16 William F. Wood, 'Chemistry of Skunk Spray', 6 October 1998, http://users.humboldt.edu.

17 Email communication from Paul Krebaum, 13 December 2013.

18 Ibid.

19 Arthur H. Howell, 'Revision of the Skunks of the Genus Spilogale', *North American Fauna*, no. 26 (Washington, DC, 1906).

20 'Coolidge Shoots Skunk in Dark as Wife Aids With Flashlight', *New York Times* (30 October 1931).

21 'Skunk Invades Diamond, Umpire Refuses to Argue', *New York Times* (9 August 1947).

22 Theodore Stankowich, Tim Caro and Matthew Cox, 'Bold Coloration and Aposematism in Terrestrial Carnivores', *Evolution*, LXV/11 (2011), pp. 3090–98.

23 Laurence Yep, *Skunk Scout* (Boston, MA, 2003), pp. 173–4.

4 COMMODIFIED SKUNK

1 See Eric Jay Dolin, *Fur, Fortune, and Empire: The Epic History of the Fur Trade in America* (New York, 2010).

2 Ibid.

3 James Churchill, *The Complete Book of Tanning Skins and Furs* (Mechanicsburg, PA, 1983), p. 33.

4 David Lantz, 'Economic Value of North American Skunks', *Farmers' Bulletin*, 587 (Washington, DC, 1917).

5 Ibid., p. 23.

6 Ibid., pp. 2, 4.

7 'Fur-ranching in England – A New Open-air Industry: A Skunk Farm on the Borders of Dartmoor', *Illustrated London News* (2 December 1922), pp. 888–9.

8 Ibid.

9 Ibid.

10 Ibid.

11 'Fur farming: A Dartmoor Experiment', *Hawera & Normanby Star*, (15 January 1923), p. 4.

12 'Odorless Skunks: Fur-farming Has Spread to British Isles', *Granby Leader-Mail* (7 March 1924).

13 Ibid.

14 'A Skunk Ranch: Daring Experiment on Dartmoor', *Singapore Free Press and Mercantile Advertiser* (8 September 1925), p. 16.

15 Ibid.

16 Ibid.

17 Fur Products Labeling Act, 15 USC § 69 passed in 1951; the 2010 amendment closes a loophole for prices under $150 and requires the label on any fur to include the following information: (1) whether the fur is natural or painted, bleached or dyed; (2) whether the product contains fur that has been sheared, plucked or let-out (optional); (3) the adjective form of the name of the country from which the animal originated (optional); (4) the name of the animal; (5) whether the fur product is composed of pieces; (6) country of origin; available at www.novacklaw.com, accessed 9 December 2014.

18 Julie Creswell, 'Real Fur Masquerading as Faux', *New York Times*, Business Day (19 March 2003); Prachi Gupta, 'Humane Society Reports that Marc Jacobs Faux Fur Coats have Real Dog Hair in them', *Salon* (8 March 2013), www.salon.com.

19 Lantz, 'Economic Value', p. 13.

20 Alberta Online Encyclopedia, 'The People of the Boreal Forest', 'Skunk', www.albertasource.ca/boreal, accessed 9 December 2014.

21 Maria del Rosario Jacobo-Salcedo, Angele Josabad Alonso-Castro and Alicia Zarate-Martinez, 'Folk Medicinal Use of Fauna in Mapimi, Durango, Mexico', *Journal of Ethnopharmacology*, CXXXIII (2011), pp. 902–6.

22 Don E. Wilson and Russell Mittermeier, eds, *Handbook of the Mammals of the World*, vol. I (Barcelona, 2009), p. 552.

23 Deborah McAleese, 'Skunk Oil Spray and Sonic Blasts to Fight Rioters', *Belfast Telegraph* (17 December 2013).

24 'Epicures Proclaim the Skunk a Tasty Dish', *New York Times* (21 December 1913).

25 Durward Allen, 'Part-time Skunkology', *Boys' Life*, 38 (March 1959).

26 Emily Andrews, 'Heaven-scent: Why Skunks are Becoming the Latest Must-have Pet', *Mail Online* (11 April 2011).

27 Ernest Thompson Seton, 'The Well Meaning Skunk', in *Wild Animals at Home* (Garden City, NY, 1913), p. 106.

28 John Burroughs, 'Real and Sham Natural History', *Atlantic Monthly*, XCI/545 (1903), p. 299.

29 Seton, 'The Well Meaning Skunk', p. 107.

30 Personal email correspondence with Deborah Cipriani, November 2013.

31 'Laments His Pet Skunk: Boy Led Animal About Up-state Village on a String', *New York Times* (21 December 1921), p. 25.

32 Constance Taber Colby, *A Skunk in the Family* (London, 1973).

5 MYTHOLOGICAL AND SPIRITUAL SKUNK

1 Bruce M. Metzger and Michael David Coogan, eds, *The Oxford Companion to the Bible* (Oxford, 1993), p. 143.

2 Isaiah 34:11; trans. from Eugene Peterson, *The Bible in Contemporary Language* (Colorado Springs, CO, 2005).

3 Vine Deloria, Jr, foreword in Michael J. Caduto and Joseph Bruchac, *Native American Animal Stories* (Golden, CO, 1992), pp. ix–xi.

4 John Bierhorst, *The Red Swan* (New York, 1976), p. 9.

5 Keeley Bassette and Rita Sharpback, retold by Richard L. Dieterle, 'Skunk Origin Myth', in *The Encyclopedia of Hočak (Winnebago) Mythology* (6 May 2010), www.hotcakencyclopedia.com.

6 Florence Reed Stratton, 'Why the Skunk Walks Alone', in *When the Storm God Rides: Tejas and Other Indian Legends* (New York, 1936, repr. 2008), p. 91.

7 William Jones, 'An Opossum Becomes Disliked Because of His Pretty Tail', in *Fox Texts* (Leyden, 1907), p. 113.

8 Ibid., pp. 113–21.

9 Laura Redish, 'Native American Skunk Mythology',
   www.native-languages.org, accessed 11 December 2014.

10 Sandy Masty, 'The Legend of Kuikuhâchâu', trans. Brian Webb,
   www.nationnews.ca, accessed 11 December 2014.

11 Hìtakonanu'laxk (Tree Beard), *The Grandfathers Speak: Native
   American Folk Tales of the Lenapé People* (New York, 1994),
   pp. 105–6.

12 'Native American Legends: The Jaguar and the Little Skunk', *First
   People: The Legends*, www.firstpeople.us., accessed 11 December
   2014.

13 John Bierhorst, *The Red Swan* (New York, 1976), p. 6.

14 Theodore Stern, 'The Trickster in Klamath Mythology', *Western
   Folklore*, XII/3 (July 1953), pp. 158–74.

15 'Skunk Outwits Coyote', *Canku Ota: A Newsletter Celebrating Native
   America* (26 August 2000), www.turtletrack.org.

16 Bobby Lake-Thom, *Spirits of the Earth: A Guide to Native American
   Nature Symbols, Stories, and Ceremonies* (New York, 1997), pp. 60–63.

17 Paul A. Johnsgard, *Lewis and Clark on the Great Plains* (Lincoln,
   NE, 2003), pp. 35–76.

18 Redish, 'Native American Skunk Mythology'.

19 Lake-Thom, *Spirits of the Earth*, pp. 94–5, 101.

20 Gladys Amanda Reichard, *An Analysis of Coeur d'Alene Indian
   Myths* (Stockbridge, MA, 2009), p. 162.

21 Michael J. Caduto and Joseph Bruchac, 'Glossary', in *Native
   American Animal Stories* (Golden, CO, 1992), p. 110.

22 Redish, 'Native American Skunk Mythology'.

23 Richard Webster, *Spirit and Dream Animals* (Woodbury, MN,
   2011), p. 3.

24 Ibid., p. 11.

25 *Oxford English Dictionary*.

26 Arlene Hirschfelder and Paulette Molin, *Encyclopedia of Native
   American Religions* (New York, 2000), pp. 306–7.

27 Ted Andrews, *Animal Speak: The Spiritual and Magical Powers of
   Creatures Great and Small* (St Paul, MN, 2000), p. 314.

28 Diane Blount-Adams, *Skunk Medicine* (Bloomington, IN, 2001), p. vii.

29 Steven D. Farmer, *Animal Spirit Guides* (New York, 2006), p. 349.
30 Steven Farmer interview with Laura Powers, Healing Powers TV, 24 July 2012.

6 NEVER CRY SKUNK

 1 David W. MacDonald, ed., *The Encyclopedia of Mammals* (Oxford, 2006), p. 508.
 2 F. Gabriel Sagard-Théodat, *Histoire du Canada* [1636], 4 vols (Paris, 1866), p. 748.
 3 'Skunk', n., *Oxford English Dictionary Online* (2013), www.oed.com.
 4 H. E. Anthony, *Mammals of America* (New York, 1917), p. 132.
 5 *OED* and various sources.
 6 Geoffrey Chaucer, 'The Pardoner's Tale', in *The Oxford Anthology of English Literature*, vol. 1 (New York, London and Toronto, 1973), p. 271.
 7 Laura A. Kiernan, 'Sen. Thurmond Calls Jenrette "Lying Skunk"', *Washington Post* (13 September 1980), p. A8. Additionally, Jenrette's self-described oversexed wife, Rita (who posed nude for *Playboy*, twice, wrote a book, and became quite a celebrity) later married Prince Nicolò Boncompagni Ludovisi of Piombino, who, in her honour, reissued a perfume that assuredly was skunk-based.
 8 William Safire, 'On Language: Garden Party Whatsit', *New York Times* (19 November 1989), p. A22.
 9 Ronald Reagan, 'Terrorist States', speech at the American Bar Association Convention, 8 July 1985, Ronald Reagan Presidential Library and Museum; available at www.reagan.utexas.edu, accessed 13 December 2013.
10 '"Skunk" Impolite', *Washington Post* (20 March 1927).
11 James Oakes, 'I Have Always Hated Slavery', in *The Radical and the Republican: Frederick Douglass, Abraham Lincoln, and the Triumph of Anti-Slavery Politics* (New York, 2007), p. 83.
12 Hans L. Trefousse, *Thaddeus Stevens, Nineteenth-century Egalitarian* (Chapel Hill, NC, 1997), p. 127.

13 *Massuere v. Dickens*, 70 Wis. 83, 35 N.W. 349, 350 (Wis. Sup. 1887).

14 'Dutch Passion – Skunk #1', Seed Finder, http://en.seedfinder.eu, accessed 13 December 2014; see also search results at www.high-times.com.

15 As of 2013 there are still a number of 'grey areas' in the level of tolerance that Dutch laws show for 'softer drugs' like marijuana. While typically prosecution is reserved for harder drugs, cannabis bans are being floated by officials.

16 John Eastman, 'Skunk-cabbage', in *The Book of Swamp and Bog: Trees, Shrubs, and Wildflowers of Eastern Freshwater Wetlands* (Mechanicsburg, PA, 1995), pp. 165–9.

17 'List of Football Club Nicknames in the United Kingdom', http://en.wikipedia.org, accessed 9 December 2014.

18 Kathleen Sykes, 'Skunk Hollow: History of a Nineteenth Century Community of Free African-Americans', *Palisades Newsletter*, 192 (March 2006).

19 Carl Sandburg, 'The Windy City', in *Smoke and Steel and Slabs of the Sunburnt West* (New York, 1922), p. 305.

20 Michael McCafferty, 'A Fresh Look at the Place Name Chicago', *Journal of the Illinois State Historical Society*, xcvi/2 (2003), p. 117.

21 Geoffrey Chaucer, 'The Knight's Tale', in *Chaucer's Canterbury Tales* (London and New York, 1903), line 403.

22 Mike Robinson, *Skunk Ape Semester* (Farmington, MO, 2011), p. 4.

23 Maurus Servius Honoratus, *Vergilii carmina comentarii*, ed. Georg Thilo and Hermann Hagen (Leipzig, 1881–1902), A.7.84; available at www.perseus.tufts.edu, accessed 13 December 2014.

24 YellowBridge Chinese Language Dictionary, www.yellowbridge.com, accessed 5 May 2013.

25 Ben Rich and Leo Janos, *Skunk Works: A Personal Memoir of My Years at Lockheed* (Boston, MA, 1996), p. 111.

26 Ibid.

27 Ibid.

1 Will Friedwald, 'Panoram Killed the Radio Star', *New York Sun* (5 March 2007).

2 Cab Calloway, 'The Skunk Song' (Minoco Productions, 1942).

3 Brecker Brothers, 'Some Skunk Funk', in *The Brecker Brothers* (Arista Records, 1975).

4 Robert Farris Thompson, *Flash of the Spirit: Afro & Afro-American Art & Philosophy* (New York, 1984), pp. 104–5.

5 Loudon Wainwright III, 'Dead Skunk (In the Middle of the Road)', *Album III* (Columbia Records, 1972).

6 Steve Huey, 'Artist Biography of Skunk Anansie', *AllMusic*, www.allmusic.com.

7 David T. Greenberg, *Skunks!* (Boston, MA, 2001).

8 Joseph T. McCann, *There's a Skunk in My Bunk* (Far Hills, NJ, 2002).

9 Shawn McMullen, *It's What's Inside that Counts* (Cincinnati, OH, 1991).

10 Libba Moore Gray, *Is There Room on the Feather Bed?* (New York, 1999).

11 Audrey Penn, *Sassafras* (Terre Haute, IN, 1995).

12 Janette Oke, *New Kid in Town* (Ada, MI, 2001), p. 69.

13 Lesléa Newman, *Skunk's Spring Surprise* (Boston, MA, 2007).

14 Stan and Jan Berenstain, *The Berenstain Bears and the Neighborly Skunk* (New York, 1984).

15 Chuck Jones, *William the Backwards Skunk* (New York, 1996).

16 *Really Scent*, dir. Abe Levitow, *Merrie Melodies*, Warner Bros (1959).

17 Robert Lowell, 'Skunk Hour', in *Collected Poems* (New York, 2006), p. 133.

18 Naomi Shahib Nye, 'A Valentine for Ernest Mann,' in *The Red Suitcase* (Rochester, NY, 2011), p. 115.

19 Seamus Heaney, 'The Skunk', in *Opened Ground: Selected Poems 1966–1996* (New York, 1998), p. 168.

20 Ibid.

21 Justin Courter, *Skunk: A Love Story* (Richmond, CA, 2007), p. 14.

22 Ibid., p. 336.

23 Mark Jenkins, 'Furry Vengeance: Skunks Aren't All That Stink', review on National Public Radio, 2010.
24 Eric Schwartz, *Sabrina Online* (1996–present), www.sabrina-online.com.

8 SKUNK SANCTUARY

1 Dove Key Ranch, http://dovekeywildlife.org, accessed 9 December 2014.
2 Personal conversations with WildCare rehabilitators, Bloomington, IN, 2011–12.
3 Emails with Deb Cipriani, autumn 2013.
4 Jerry W. Dragoo and R. L. Honeycutt, 'Systematics of Mustelid-like Carnivores', *Journal of Mammalogy*, LXXVIII (1997), pp. 426–43, and Eduardo Eizirik, et al., 'Pattern and Timing of Diversification of the Mammalian Order Carnivora Inferred from Multiple Nuclear Gene Sequences', *Molecular Phylogenetics and Evolution*, LVI/1 (July 2010), pp. 49–63.
5 Exotic Pet Awareness Day (Facebook page), www.facebook.com/pages/Exotic-Pet-Awareness-Day; see also www.petskunks.co.uk, accessed 9 December 2014.
6 Stichting Het Stinkdier, www.stichtinghetstinkdier.nl, accessed 9 December 2014.
7 World Health Organization (WHO), www.who.int/.
8 Ibid.
9 Dragoo Institute for the Betterment of Skunks and Skunk Reputations, http://dragoo.org, accessed 8 December 2014.
10 'Shot for a Skunk', *New York Times* (9 November 1884), p. 5.
11 'Gunning for Skunk, Man Kills Wife', *New York Times* (16 October 1928), p. 33.
12 Associated Press, 'PA Girl in Costume Mistaken for Skunk, Shot' (22 October 2012), www.cbsnews.com, accessed 15 December 2014.

Select Bibliography

Allen, Joel Asaph, 'The Generic Names of the Mephitinae',
    Bulletin of the American Museum of Natural History, XIV (1901),
    pp. 325–34
Anthony, H.E., *Mammals of America* (New York, 1917)
Asúa, Miguel de, and Roger French, *A New World of Animals: Early
    Modern Europeans on the Creatures of Iberian America* (Aldershot
    and Burlington, VT, 2005)
Bassette, Keeley (Waterspirit Clan), and Rita Sharpback (Buffalo
    Clan), 'How Skunks Came to Be', in *Folklore of the Winnebago
    Tribe*, ed. David Lee Smith (Norman, OK, 1997)
——, and ——, retold by Richard L. Dieterle, 'Skunk Origin Myth',
    The Encyclopedia of Hočak (Winnebago) Mythology (6 May 2010),
    www.hotcakencyclopedia.com
Caduto, Michael J., and Joseph Bruchac, *Native American Animal
    Stories* (Golden, CO, 1992)
Darwin, Charles, *A Naturalist's Voyage Around the World* [*Voyage of the
    Beagle*] (1839) (London, 1860), p. 83
——, *Journal of Research into the Geology and Natural History of the
    Various Counties Visited by HMS 'Beagle'* (London, 1839), entry for
    23 August 1833
Dolin, Eric Jay, *Fur, Fortune, and Empire* (New York, 2010)
Dragoo, J. W., and R. L. Honeycutt, 'Systematics of Mustelid-like
    Carnivores', *Journal of Mammalogy*, LXVIII (1997), pp. 426–43
Hirschfelder, Arlene, and Paulette Molin, *Encyclopedia of Native
    American Religions* (New York, 2000)

Hìtakonanu'laxk (Tree Beard), *The Grandfathers Speak: Native American Folk Tales of the Lenapé People* (New York, 1994)

Howell, Arthur H., 'Revision of the Skunks of the Genus Spilogale', *North American Fauna*, 26 (1906)

Is That Skunk?, John Rubin Productions, Inc. and Thirteen in association with wnet.org (25 January 2009). Available on DVD or online (U.S. only) at www.pbs.org

Lake-Thom, Bobby, *Spirits of the Earth: A Guide to Native American Nature Symbols, Stories, and Ceremonies* (New York, 1997)

Lantz, David, 'Economic Value of North American Skunks', *Farmers' Bulletin*, 587 (Washington, DC, 1917)

Lawson, John, *A New Voyage to Carolina; Containing the Exact Description and Natural History of that Country: Together with the Present State Thereof. And a Journal of a Thousand Miles, Travel'd Thro' Several Nations of Indians. Giving a Particular Account of their Customs, Manners, &c.* (London, 1709)

Lewis, Meriwether, and William Clark, *Journals of the Lewis and Clark Expedition Online*, http://lewisandclarkjournals.unl.edu, accessed 15 October 2013

Macdonald, David W., ed., 'Skunks and Stink Badgers', in *The Encyclopedia of Mammals* (Oxford, 2006)

Masty, Sandy, 'The Legend of Kuikuhâchâu', trans. Brian Webb (6 January 2005), www.beesum-communications.com

Molina, Juan Ignacio, *The Geographical, Natural and Civil History of Chili* [trans. R. Alsop], 2 vols (Middletown, CT, 1808)

'Native American Legends: The Jaguar and the Little Skunk', *First People: The Legends*, www.firstpeople.us, accessed 11 December 2014

Redish, Laura, 'Native American Skunk Mythology', www.native-languages.org

Reichard, Gladys Amanda, *An Analysis of Coeur d'Alene Indian Myths* (Stockbridge, MA, 2009)

Robinson, Mike, *Skunk Ape Semester* (Farmington, MO, 2012)

Schiaffini, M. I., et al., 'Taxonomic status of Southern South American *Conepatus* (Carnivora: Mephitidae)', *Zoological Journal of the Linnaean Society*, CLXVII (2013), pp. 327–44

Schreber, Johann, *Die Säugthiere in Abbildungen nach der Natur mit Beschreibungen*, 7 vols (Erlangen, 1774–1846)

Stankowich, Theodore, Tim Caro and Matthew Cox, 'Bold Coloration and Aposematism in Terrestrial Carnivores', *Evolution*, LXV/11 (2011), pp. 3090–98

Stern, Theodore, 'The Trickster in Klamath Mythology', *Western Folklore*, XII/3 (July 1953), pp. 158–74

Stratton, Florence Reed, 'Why the Skunk Walks Alone', in *When the Storm God Rides: Tejas and Other Indian Legends* (New York, 1936, repr. 2008)

Wang, X., D. P. Whistler and G. T. Takeuchi, 'A New Basal Skunk *Martinogale* (Carnivora, Mephitinae) from late Miocene Dove Spring Formation, California and Origin of New World mephitines', *Journal of Vertebrate Paleontology*, XXV/4 (2005), pp. 936–49

Wang, Xiaoming, 'Passing the Smell Test', *Natural History*, CXX/5 (May 2012), pp. 22–9

Webster, Richard, *Spirit and Dream Animals* (Woodbury, MN, 2011)

Whitaker, John O., Jr., and Russell E. Mumford, *Mammals of Indiana* (Bloomington, IN, 2009)

Wilson, Don E., and DeeAnn M. Reeder, *Mammal Species of the World: A Taxonomic and Geographic Reference*, 3rd edn (Baltimore, MD, 2005)

——, and Russell Mittermeier, eds, *Handbook of the Mammals of the World*, vol. I (Barcelona, 2009), p. 552

——, and Sue Ruff, 'Family Mephitidae', in *The Smithsonian Book of North American Mammals* (Washington, DC, and London, 1999)

Wood, William F., 'The History of Skunk Defensive Secretion Research', *Chemical Educator*, IV/2 (1999), pp. 44–50

Associations and Websites

BUSCH WILDLIFE SANCTUARY
www.buschwildlife.org/animals/animals.skunks.html

DRAGOO INSTITUTE FOR THE BETTERMENT OF SKUNKS AND SKUNK
REPUTATIONS
http://dragoo.org

THE HUMANE SOCIETY OF THE UNITED STATES
www.humanesociety.org/animals/skunks

NATIVE ANIMAL RESCUE
www.nativeanimalrescue.org/found-an-animal/skunks

ORPHANED WILDLIFE CARE
www.orphanedwildlifecare.com/skunkcare.htm

OWNERS OF PET SKUNKS (OOPS)
www.skunk-info.org

'PET SKUNKS FOR SALE' BLOG
http://skunkiedelight.wordpress.com/category/pet-skunks

SKUNK HAVEN
www.skunkhaven.net

SOCIETY OF KIND UNDERSTANDING AND NOT KILLING SKUNKS
www.stinkybusiness.org

THE SKUNK WHISPERER
http://totalwildlifecontrol.com/live-trapping-and-relocation

VINTAGE FASHION GUILD
http://vintagefashionguild.org/fur-resource/skunk

WALKIN' WILD SKUNK RESCUE
www.wildskunkrescue.com

Acknowledgements

A number of people helped to move this book along, contributing to the research and fleshing out of information, but the deepest gratitude goes to my ever-patient and brilliant brother Mark Miller, who read the entire manuscript several times, and whose tireless research acumen and painstaking editorial skills helped bring this book to life.

I also would like to thank skunk advocate Deb Cipriani, whose devotion to and knowledge of skunks is unmatched, and to all the folks at Skunkfest 2013 who shared their stories (and their skunks) with me during a wonderful day.

Special thanks also goes to WildCare in Bloomington, Indiana, and the wildlife rehabilitator who provided me with an afternoon of skunk-filled entertainment in my own backyard.

Thanks to Indiana University and the English department for the semester sabbatical that allowed me time to focus on the project, as well as appreciation to several helpful librarians and faculty on campus. A well-deserved acknowledgement also goes to Debora Shaw, friend and expert indexer, who shouldered so much of the weight of this task. Thanks are of course extended to the hard-working crew at Reaktion, especially Michael Leaman, Harry Gilonis and Amy Salter. My appreciation also goes to Jonathan Burt, editor of the Animal Series, whose cheerful suggestions and humour smoothed the way.

I also thank all those, strangers and friends, who, upon learning I was writing a book on skunks, began sending me photos, anecdotes and questions, demonstrating their newfound appreciation for these beautiful animals.

Most specifically, this book is dedicated to my beautiful sister, Letitia Ann Elizabeth Miller, who unexpectedly left this world and a huge hole in my heart before the book was finished. Her magical compassion for and understanding of all animals served as a guide.

PERMISSIONS

Naomi Shihab Nye, excerpt from 'Valentine for Ernest Mann' from *Red Suitcase*. Copyright © 1994 by Naomi Shihab Nye. Reprinted with the permission of The Permissions Company, Inc., on behalf of BOA Editions, Ltd., www.boaeditions.org.

Photo Acknowledgements

The author and publishers wish to express their thanks to the below sources of illustrative material and/or permission to reproduce it:

Photo © 4loops/iStock International Inc.: p. 137; ArtPixz/Bigstock-Photo: p. 72; from J. W. Audubon, *The Quadrupeds of North America*: pp. 99 (vol. I – New York, 1851–4), 109 (vol. II – New York, 1851); collection of the author, gift from the artist (Alexis Wreden): p. 98; courtesy of the author: pp. 11, 13, 33, 47, 48, 54, 55, 89, 112, 113, 135, 139, 140, 144, 147, 148, 156, 160, 161, 164; from Thomas Bewick, *A General History of Quadrupeds* (Newcastle-upon-Tyne, 1790): p. 18; photo Martin Bravenboer: p. 126; from A. E. Brehm, *Het Leven der Dieren*, vol. IV (Zutphen, 1927): p. 49; British Museum, London (photos © The Trustees of the British Museum): pp. 18, 142; from Mark Catesby, *The Natural History of Carolina, Florida and the Bahama Islands*, vol. II (London, 1754): p. 27; photo © Gclick/iStock International Inc.: p. 8; from Oliver Goldsmith, *An History of the Earth, and Animated Nature*, vol. III (London, 1774): p. 94; photo © goosey270/iStock International Inc.: p. 73; from David Greenberg, *Skunks!* (Boston, 2004): p. 140; from *Illustrations of Zoology: The Engravings by J. W. Lowry and T. Landseer: With descriptive Letterpress embracing a systematic View of the Animal Kingdom, according to Cuvier, with characteristic anecdotes and narratives . . .* (London and Glasgow, 1851): p. 24; from D. M. Kelsey, *The New World heroes of discovery and conquest* (Philadelphia, 1891): p. 21; photo Brian Kentosh: p. 45; from Ferdinand Krauss, *Die Säugethiere nach Familien und Gattungen . . .* (Stuttgart and Esslingen, 1851): p. 28; photo © Lambada/iStock

International Inc.: p. 68; from David Lantz, *Economic Value of North American Skunks* (Washington, DC, 1917): p. 83; photo LeatherBagLady, reproduced by kind permission: p. 100; from Georges-Louis Leclerc, Comte de Buffon, *Histoire Naturelle, Générale et Particuliére . . .* (Paris, 1845): p. 26; photos Library of Congress, Washington, DC: pp. 16, 21, 22, 79; from Hinrich Lichtenstein, *Darstellung neuer und wenig bekannter Säugethiere in Abbildungen und Beschreibungen . . .* (Berlin, 1827–34): pp. 36, 37, 40; photo Lynn_B/BigstockPhoto: p. 9; photo Alyce Miller and Ann Gerster: p. 159; photo © mindi_jean/iStock International Inc.: p. 6; Muzeum Czartoryski, Kraków: p. 151; National Anthropological Archives, Smithsonian Museum Support Centre, Suitland, Maryland: p. 106; photo Neftali/BigstockPhoto: p. 111; reproduced courtesy of University of Minnesota Libraries, Manuscripts Division, Minneapolis: p. 120; from Edward W. Nelson, *Wild Animals of North America: Intimate Studies of Big and Little Creatures of the Mammal Kingdom* (Washington, DC, 1918) pp. 29, 34, 50, 102; from Alcide d'Orbigny, *Voyage dans l'Amérique méridionale (le Brésil, la république orientale de l'Uruguay, la République argentine, la Patagonie, la république du Chili, la république de Bolivia, la république du Pérou), exécuté pendant les années 1826, 1827, 1828, 1829, 1830, 1831, 1832, et 1833* (Paris and Strasbourg, 1835): p. 41; photo Edgar Samuel Paxon: p. 23; photo by and reproduced courtesy of Ann Peters: p. 165; Alan and Vicena Poulson/BigstockPhoto: p. 154; photo © raciro/iStock International Inc.: p. 19; Rex Features/Everett Collection: p. 76; photo E. T. Seton, from Ernest Thompson Seton, *Wild Animals at Home* (London, 1913): p. 87; Sid Richardson Museum, Fort Worth, Texas: p. 58; photo Skimsta: p. 35; from Charles Hamilton Smith, *Mammalia*, vol. xv in William Jardine, ed., *The Naturalist's Library* (Edinburgh, 1845–6): p. 32; from Joseph Wolf, *Zoological Sketches by Joseph Wolf: Made for the Zoological Society of London, from Animals in their Vivarium, in the Regent's Park* (London, 1861): p. 105; photos © Zoological Society of London: pp. 24, 26, 27, 28, 32, 36, 37, 40, 94, 105, 109.

Jef Poskanzer, the copyright holder of the image on p. 65, has published this online under conditions imposed by a Creative Commons Attribution 2.0 Generic license; payayita, the copyright holder of the

Index